the (UN)HAPPY lawyer

A Roadmap
to Finding
Meaningful Work
Outside of
the Law

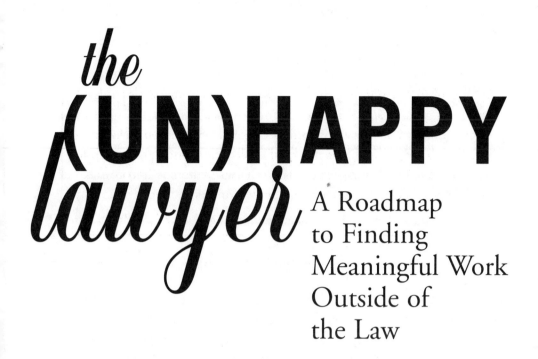

the (UN)HAPPY lawyer

A Roadmap
to Finding
Meaningful Work
Outside of
the Law

Monica R. Parker, JD

SPHINX® PUBLISHING
AN IMPRINT OF SOURCEBOOKS, INC.®
NAPERVILLE, ILLINOIS
www.SphinxLegal.com

Published by: **Sphinx® Publishing, An Imprint of Sourcebooks, Inc.®**

Naperville Office
P.O. Box 4410
Naperville, Illinois 60567-4410
(630) 961-3900
Fax: 630-961-2168
www.sourcebooks.com
www.SphinxLegal.com

This publication is designed to provide accurate and authoritative information in regard to the subject matter covered. It is sold with the understanding that the publisher is not engaged in rendering legal, accounting, or other professional service. If legal advice or other expert assistance is required, the services of a competent professional person should be sought.

From a Declaration of Principles Jointly Adopted by a Committee of the American Bar Association and a Committee of Publishers and Associations

This product is not a substitute for legal advice.

Disclaimer required by Texas statutes.

Library of Congress Cataloging-in-Publication Data

Parker, Monica (Monica R.)
   The unhappy lawyer : a roadmap to finding meaningful work outside of the law / by Monica Parker. -- 1st ed.
      p. cm.
   Includes bibliographical references and index.
   ISBN 978-1-57248-670-6 (pbk. : alk. paper) 1. Career changes. 2. Career changes--Case studies. 3. Vocational guidance. 4. Lawyers. I. Title.
   HF5384.P37 2008
   331.702--dc22
                                    2008018159

Printed and bound in the United States of America.
VP 10 9 8 7 6 5 4 3 2 1

Acknowledgments

Thank you to my parents, Merita and Gregg Parker, and my brothers, Walter and Parke Parker (yes, that's his name, Walter and I got to help name him), for supporting me throughout all the twists and turns of my careers.

Inexpressible gratitude for Cynthia Morris, coach extraordinaire and one of my staunchest supporters.

Much appreciation for my clients and all the lawyers who have spilled out their hearts' desires to me. This book is for you.

Thank you to Jacqueline Hackett, Esq., my agent and a partner in crime in leaving the practice of law.

Thank you to Erin Shanahan, Esq., my editor and another partner in crime who wisely avoided the practice of law altogether.

Thank you to Chuck Adams, Debbie Goldstein, Amy Gutman, Carolyn Pitt-Jones, Cheryl Schneider, Voltaire Sterling, Victoria Sanders, Erica Hashimoto, Vivian Wexler, and Jennifer Alvey for so generously sharing your stories. Thank you for confirming my belief that the pursuit of happiness in your work is a worthy and necessary goal.

I would also like to give thanks to God, Father of our Savior, the Lord Jesus Christ. I am so blessed to have this opportunity to do work that I love and to touch others' lives.

Monica R. Parker
December 1, 2007
Atlanta, GA

"Well if I can't be a cowboy I'll be a lawyer for cowboys."

A Few Words about Confidentiality

As a career coach, I respect the confidentiality of my work with my clients. So the stories you will read here aren't me breaking that confidence; they are illustrative examples. Except for the "Letter from a Desperate Lawyer" segments and "Case Studies," these are not real people or real events. All names have been changed.

Contents

What Do You Want?
What's Your Ideal Day, Other than Calling in Sick to Stay in Bed All Day?
What Interests You Other than Earning an Income?
What Talents Do You Have, Other than Researching, Doing Document
    Reviews, and Filing Briefs?
What Career Possibilities Excite You, Other than Taking a Sabbatical?
You Did It!
Appreciate Uncertainty
Case Study: Debbie Goldstein, Managing Director of Triad Consulting Group
What You Should Have Learned in this Chapter

Who Are You Spending Your Time With?
Make Some New Friends
Support Group
The Buddy System
Hire a Coach
Case Study: Voltaire Sterling, Stage and Screen Actor, Producer, Philanthropist
What You Should Have Learned in this Chapter

Give Yourself Permission to Screw Up
The Point
Give Yourself Permission to Change Your Mind
Give Yourself Permission to Change Careers
Give Yourself Permission to Do Work You Love
Case Study: Chuck Adams, Executive Editor
What You Should Have Learned in this Chapter

A Note from the Author

I KNOW JUST HOW YOU FEEL

I earned a BA from Harvard College and a JD from Harvard Law School. I had my choice of six-figure law firm positions and chose to go practice at a prestigious large law firm. I thought I had it made. To my shock and dismay, I realized I didn't enjoy practicing law.

I tried to stick with my profession. I really did. I tried to convince myself that it wasn't the practice of law I didn't like—it was my job. So I considered changing to another practice group or maybe going to another firm. I ended up doing both—I switched to a small firm and completely changed practice areas.

A year later, I was just as miserable as I was at my first firm. Dreading going to work. Cringing when a partner came by my office with a new assignment. Even my body had started rejecting my job—I was getting pounding headaches almost every other day.

That's when I realized it was time to admit to myself that I didn't need a new legal job—I needed to get out of the law altogether.

I DECIDED TO GET SERIOUS AND FIND MY DREAM JOB

Friends had laughed at how focused I was the first time I explored changing jobs. Now they were concerned because I was obsessed.

I read all the career development books at the bookstore. I did every career exploration exercise I could find. I took scads of career assessment tests. I signed up for an extensive (and expensive) career course. As you can imagine, I spent a lot of money, time, energy, tears, and prayers on my mission.

Five years later, I'd figured out some possibilities but still didn't know how I was going to make the transition. I'd learned a lot about myself, but nothing had changed. I was still plodding into my law office every day.

I was waiting for the heavens to open up, a thunderbolt to crack, and lightning to illuminate my path—or even a bus to sideswipe me gently enough to put me out of commission for six months or so.

That's when it hit me. (No, not a bus!)

I WAS WAITING FOR SOMETHING TO HAPPEN, INSTEAD OF MAKING SOMETHING HAPPEN

You see, I'd always been a woman of action. If I wanted to do something, I did it. I didn't sit around thinking about how much I wanted it and doing nothing. I went after it and always succeeded.

For example, in college, I took over a tired dance company and revitalized it. I started a new a cappella group that was an unprecedented success. I approached Spike Lee for a job, and he hired me after a three-month internship.

I was fearless. So what in the world had happened to me?

I WENT TO LAW SCHOOL

Law school? Yes, that coveted law school education had stifled me.

Just think about it. I was highly trained in risk aversion. I had spent three years studying the wreckage created, fortunes lost, and lives destroyed by people and entities taking action.

In addition, I'd spent five years practicing law, which only reinforced my mind-set that taking action—any action—was highly risky.

I didn't dare put my toe in the water of career change for fear that a piranha might gnaw my leg off.

THAT'S WHEN I REALIZED THE RIGHT SIDE OF MY BRAIN HAD ATROPHIED

That glorious, daring side of my brain that had propelled me through an engaging, meaningful, fulfilling college career had withered away. I needed to find some way to build it back up.

I knew there were no career development programs like that out there. Trust me, I looked. So, I decided I was going to have to create one myself.

I did, and, within ten months, I slammed the door shut on my less-than-fulfilling legal career to pursue the career of my dreams.

Are you ready to do the same?

Seven Reasons to Leave the Practice of Law—and What You Will Find on the Other Side

DO YOU WANT TO LEAVE THE PRACTICE OF LAW BUT WONDER IF IT'S FOR THE RIGHT REASONS?

If so, you're in the right place because you're going to read all the secrets that unhappy lawyers keep about how they feel about practicing law.

I struggled with the same question myself when I practiced law. And now as a career coach helping unhappy lawyers find fulfilling work outside the practice of law, I find that a lot of lawyers grapple with this question. I'm glad that I can share our experiences with you.

But that's not all you want to know. You want to know if you will be happy and successful if you leave.

You have already accomplished a great deal. You finished law school, took the bar, and started practicing. You may not find it to be engaging work, but at least you have a steady, prestigious job that pays well. What if you leave and it's a big mistake?

Look at how successful you were at becoming a lawyer. Imagine how successful you would be if you put your energy and passion into work that you love.

HOW TO GET THE MOST OUT OF THIS BOOK

Are you coachable? If you are in a stubborn frame of mind, want to do things your own way, and are not open to ideas, then you're not going to get much out of this book. But let me ask you this—how well is that approach working for you? Maybe it's time to try something different.

Are you willing to:

- be open to new ideas and new ways of being;

- let go of self-sabotaging attitudes and behaviors;

- accept responsibility for your life and your work;

- maintain your sense of humor throughout this process; and,

- hear the truth, even if it's a hard truth?

If you answered these questions in the affirmative, then you're in the right place! The coaching relationship works because the coach and client grant it the power to work. Sure, we're not working in person together, but we can have that same kind of powerful coaching relationship through this book. Read it and make a commitment to explore what fulfilling work would look like for you.

DO ANY OF THESE SEVEN REASONS TO LEAVE THE PRACTICE OF LAW APPLY TO YOU?

Reason #1: Everyone Else's Job Looks Fascinating

You are really good at romanticizing everyone else's job. You see a postal worker drive up to your mailbox and think, "That must be such a peaceful job. You're working on your own, just dropping mail in the boxes, nobody to bother you."

Before I stopped practicing law, I was fascinated by the landscaping company at my law firm's building, the bakery truck that passed me on the way to work, the building across the street—I thought, "I wonder what they do there?"

If you are longing to take *anyone* else's job in place of your own, it's time to take your dissatisfaction seriously. When you're doing work that you love, you rarely fantasize about having someone else's job.

Reason #2: You're Doing the Sunday Night Countdown

If you don't like practicing law, Sunday is a hard day. The day goes by much too quickly. All of a sudden, it's 6:00 p.m., and you realize you only have six more hours left in your weekend. You eat dinner at 7:00 p.m. and note that you only have five more hours. You're watching your favorite television show at 9:00...and you're not just watching the clock; you get more depressed as the day wears on.

This is *not* normal.

When I left the law, Sunday turned back into what Sunday was meant to be—a day of rest and pleasurable anticipation about what the week would bring.

Reason #3: You're Bored or Overwhelmed

Unhappy lawyers move back and forth between being bored senseless and feeling overwhelmed by their work. When you don't have enough work, you realize just how uninterested you are in the intricacies of the law. And it's not any better to have too much to do. Then you're just stressed about how you're going to get all of this complicated stuff done.

This pattern was a big problem for me. I would be hard-pressed to tell you about a project that didn't either put me to sleep or make me gnaw my nails off from the anxiety. I didn't expect work to be as much fun as going to Disney World, but this level of stress didn't seem right either. Work should be engaging with just enough challenge.

Reason #4: You Feel Like an Imposter

You made it through law school. You passed the bar exam. You're practicing law. Anyone looking in on this scene would think that you are a confident, capable individual.

You, on the other hand, are pretty sure that today is the day that a partner will walk into your office and expose you as a phony.

It doesn't matter how many years you practice. The doubts and insecurities don't go away. You wonder what's wrong with you. Nothing's wrong with you. You have the *wrong job*.

When you find work that's right for you, the pieces of the puzzle fall into place. The doubts don't go away completely, but rather than overwhelming you, they're a buzz in the background where they belong.

Reason #5: You Couldn't Care Less about Your Performance

Tell me if this description of your last annual review is accurate.

> *The partner (or your supervisor) spent the obligatory thirty seconds talking about what you've done well, but mainly he talked about what you need to do to improve. What were you thinking while he was droning on? "I have no interest in what you're saying."*

When you enjoy what you do, it matters to you whether you are doing your work well. If you're not interested in improving your performance, you are not doing the right work.

Reason #6: You're Sabotaging Yourself

You test the boundaries. You barely make your billable hours, or you don't make them at all. You do the work, but you take a lot longer than necessary to complete it. Maybe you do just enough to get by.

Perhaps you surf the Web (and don't care if your firm is monitoring your use), or you visit with coworkers, or you look for any excuse to leave the office—getting your eyebrows waxed, taking your car in to be serviced, getting a root canal.

When your work engages you, you don't need to test the boundaries. I no longer feel compelled to keep up with the entertainment section of MSN.com or instantly open every interesting email I receive.

Reason #7: You Don't Like Practicing Law

Amazingly simple, isn't it? When you were a kid, if you didn't like what you were doing, you stopped and did something else. You didn't analyze or doubt what you felt.

Why is it that, as adults, we lose the ability to trust our instincts? Instead, we say, "I wish I could quit but I have no idea what I want to do. What if I can't find anything? What if what I want to do doesn't pay enough?"

But what if you find work that is engaging *and* financially rewarding?

CONCLUSION

Did you see your reasons for wanting to leave the practice of law on the list? If so, it's time to explore what would be fulfilling work for you.

Do you have different reasons for wanting to leave? Those are good reasons, too. If you can't shake your dissatisfaction with the practice of law, that's enough of a reason to explore alternative careers.

So, what will it be? You can finish this book and go back to your legal research, or you can make a commitment to finding happiness and success in your career.

You have tremendous gifts and talents. You deserve to use them in work that fulfills you. Imagine what a blessing that will be for you when you do.

chapter one

For Desperate Lawyers Who Don't Have a Clue What They Want to Do

---

LETTER FROM A DESPERATE LAWYER

Dear Monica,

Maybe I could get hit by a bus and end up in a coma. I don't want to be permanently injured, just incapacitated. Six months to a year would be good. That should give me plenty of time to think about what else I want to do.

Rose

Sound familiar? Step away from the curb. This chapter will guide you to meaningful work that excites you, allows you to be yourself, and gives you your life back—rather than taking it away, which is where you're headed with the getting-hit-by-a-bus strategy.

The first step to leaving the law is usually the most challenging part for lawyers—figuring out which options catch your eye. The trick is to distract the left brain so that the right brain can come out and play in an uninhibited fashion.

How do you do that? I've got solutions to that problem in this chapter. It is full of exercises designed to circumvent the left brain and let you dream, imagine, and create, just like when you were a kid.

WHAT DO YOU WANT?

Figuring out what you want is a crucial first step in finding fulfilling work outside the law. It reminds you of who you were before law school.

When I ask my clients, "What do you want?" their first response is often silence. Most of us don't have a clue. We knew we wanted to go to law school, but after that it gets hazy. Once we got there, the law school mentality and competitiveness took over and the focus became getting good grades, getting interviews with the best, highest paying firms, and getting offers. Any other dreams and desires took a backseat to this narrow definition of success.

All that is fine until you're sitting at your desk at the firm one day and realize you're desperately unhappy with what you do. You can tell me what you don't want, but you don't have any idea what you do want.

Grab a notebook and a pen, and let's get started.

Answer these questions.

- What do you want for yourself?

- What are you willing to do to have it?

These are open-ended questions. Tell me what you want for your work and your life. My clients, when given the go-ahead, tell me absolutely anything they want—they share what they want from work, from life, from love, from the bully who stole their lunch box in third grade. Take a few minutes to jot down your answers.

To help you get started with your own answers, look at what Margaret, a fifth-year associate at a large firm, wrote:

> *I just want to know that my work has meaning. That I'm helping individuals improve their lives, not corporations improve their bottom line. I'd like some laughter, to get up in the morning looking forward to work. To work with people I love and who care very deeply about me.*

Are you surprised by what you wrote for your own answers? Dismayed that your life as it is now doesn't remotely reflect your dreams? These are common, expected reactions.

Post your answers somewhere you can see them every day—on your refrigerator, in a (locked) desk drawer at work, on a bulletin board in your home office, in your secret candy stash drawer.

Why? Because once you begin dreaming about the possibilities, your internal voice begins its attack: "Are you sure you want to do this? What are you thinking? You can't leave your job. Are you kidding?" Don't try to argue with your internal voice. Instead, reread your answers to these questions. They will remind you what is important to you and why making this change is worth it.

WHAT'S YOUR IDEAL DAY, OTHER THAN CALLING IN SICK TO STAY IN BED ALL DAY?

No, you can't have your ideal day every day. On the other hand, you're probably going to continue to have nothing but less-than-ideal days if you don't at least try to figure out what your ideal day looks like.

Now is the time to do some free writing. Get comfortable, set a timer for fifteen minutes, put your pen on the paper, and write what your vision of your ideal day is without lifting your pen until the timer buzzes. If you don't know what to say, go ahead and write, "I don't know what to say," over and over again until you do know what to say. Write in the present tense (i.e., "I wake to the sound of birds chirping in my backyard rather than my alarm clock").

Here are a few questions to get you started.

- What time do you wake up?

- Where do you live? (Describe your home and your neighborhood.)

- What do you do when you get up?

- What time do you go to work?

- Who are you working with, if anyone?

- What does your work space look like?

- Are you at your office all day, or are you going other places?

- What do those other places look like?

- Do you have clients? What are they like?

- What time do you leave work?

- What do you do after you leave?

- What time do you go to bed?

Be colorful. Be descriptive. Create a vivid picture with your words—something you can see, smell, taste, and touch.

Post your answers to these questions where you can see them every day, as well. Your ideal day description can be so inspirational to reread, especially on a bad day.

My clients also use it to evaluate a career change. If the new career you're contemplating doesn't give you the opportunity to live out a good chunk of your ideal day, that realization should tell you something.

WHAT INTERESTS YOU OTHER THAN EARNING AN INCOME?

I like this exercise because it goes back to the basics—*what engages you?* Don't know anymore? That's okay. We'll figure it out.

This exercise requires patience because it takes at least six to eight weeks. Get a small notebook—one that will fit in your pocket or your purse. You want to have it with you every day.

Let's start with the past. Remember your childhood, adolescence, and college years. What interested you? Write it all down in your notebook. If your memory isn't so good, check in with your family. They'll be delighted to remind you of the theatrical productions you directed, produced, and starred in when you were 8 years old wearing your Wonder Woman costume, your older sister's red boots, and a cape.

Then, write down what interests you now. Write down five to ten things in your notebook. Then continue with the exercise because we'll need a *lot* more to work with than that. Aim for fifty interests over the next several weeks. For the next six to eight weeks, every time something catches your interest, pull out your notebook and write it down. Here are some ideas.

- Jealous of a pastry chef you read about in a magazine article who has a dessert café and travels around the world for sweet inspiration? Write it down.

- Interested in signing up for a kickboxing class? Write it down.

- Saw a commercial about the white sand beaches of Turks and Caicos and started drooling?

- Bought a new book that you couldn't put down, so you ended up oversleeping the next day?

- Overheard a conversation at Starbucks and almost fell out of your chair trying to eavesdrop?

- Enamored with a TV show?

- Daydreaming about owning that beautiful flower shop that just opened around the corner?

- Saw Cirque de Soleil yesterday, and keep having thoughts that you wish you could be involved with the company in some way?

Don't just write the item down, though. Jot down a few words about what appeals to you about the item. So, in addition to "pastry chef," include "chocolate, entrepreneur, customers lined up out the door, travel to exotic locales, creative."

Absolutely no analysis is allowed while you're completing this exercise. Don't think that something is too crazy to do. Just write down whatever appeals to you.

After six to eight weeks, take a look at your scribbles. Do you have at least fifty items in your notebook? If so, proceed to the next step.

If not, either you've forgotten to take your notebook with you and relying on your memory isn't working, or you're not getting out enough. If it's the former, give yourself two more weeks and make sure you've got your notebook with you at all times so you can capture everything. If it's the latter, take two more weeks and explore!

Here are a few ideas to get you going.

- Read continuing education catalogues.

- Wander around a bookstore/music store/video store and pick up anything that appeals to you.

- Commandeer your TV remote and channel surf.

- Mercilessly eavesdrop at every possible opportunity.

- List people you're jealous of.

- Hang around with your kids or borrow someone else's—they've got terrific imaginations.

Once you've got fifty interests or more, it's time to sort them. What connections do you see between the interests? Sort them into five to ten categories. Then create titles for each of those categories. Be creative and descriptive—it can be one word or a string of words. If you're having trouble with this step, enlist a friend to help you. Type up a list of your category titles and the interests under each category.

As an example, here are some of the categories Giselle, a third-year government lawyer, came up with.

- Cooking for entertaining

- Self-improvement

- Experimental education

- Relaxation/meditation/recharging

- Dance/movement/challenging physical activity

- Passion—finding it, being immersed in it for work/genius

- Quirky/silly/trashy novels

QUICK TIP

Just can't bear to wait six to eight weeks to uncover your interests? All right, you instant gratification junkie. The fastest way I know to do this is to spend two to three hours browsing at a large bookstore. Head to your usual favorite sections and select whatever appeals to you, but then also take a tour around the rest of the store and pick up whatever catches your eye (including books in the children's section). Do the same with the magazine section, the DVD section, and the CD section. Jot down everything that gets your attention, and you should have a pretty big list to play with.

WHAT TALENTS DO YOU HAVE, OTHER THAN RESEARCHING, DOING DOCUMENT REVIEWS, AND FILING BRIEFS?

There's a problem with being bright. When you're bright, it means that you're good at a lot of things. But it doesn't mean that you like doing them. It's time to distinguish between what you do and don't like to do.

What Are Your Talents?

When I ask this question, the room gets so silent I can hear crickets chirping. Lawyers are notorious for being unaware of their talents. They're positive they're only good at one thing—the skills that are required for being a good lawyer.

Of course, this is not very likely. By *talents* I'm referring to your natural abilities, not necessarily the skills you've acquired along the way in your career. It's the stuff you find easy to do, often to the extent that others marvel at your capability.

Bob McDonald and Don Hutcheson define talents in their book *Don't Waste Your Talent: The 8 Critical Steps to Discovering What You Do Best* as follows:

> Every one of us is born with unique talents and gifts. They are hardwired into us. We don't learn them and we can't forget them. They are just part of who we are. For some, talents are specialized and particular—a gift for music or design, for instance, or a gift for theoretical thought. For others, talents are more generalized—as a talent for leading teams, or abilities that make teaching, selling, or writing easy.[1]

Sadly enough, most of my clients haven't used their talents in so long that they've forgotten what they are. That's okay; there are lots of different ways you can uncover your talents. The following are two of my favorite approaches.

1. **The assessment way.** There are some incredibly insightful assessments available today. I'm not talking about the ones that spit out a list of careers for you to choose from. Be wary of those. As wonderful as it would be to have a computer tell you what to do, you are the best judge of that. I'm talking about assessments that help you identify your natural aptitudes, like the *Highlands Ability Battery*. Highlands not only assesses your talents, but also identifies which ones you absolutely have to use in order to have satisfaction in your work.

Some of the most powerful and influential talents are what McDonald and Hutcheson call *Driving Abilities*: "Driving Abilities…influence or drive you whether they are high or low. If you ignore them, you run the significant risk of getting into a role that doesn't use your strongest talent or that loads on a talent you don't have. [A] great deal of dissatisfaction can be traced to having strong talents that you never use."[2]

Here's what I discovered about my Driving Abilities when I took Highlands:

- My *Idea Productivity* score: High.
  I have a large number of ideas flowing through my head at any one time. I cannot turn this ability off at will. The more I am in situations in which I need to come up with new ideas and new ways of looking at things, the happier I'll be.

- My *Classification* score: Low.
  I solve problems in a linear way, whereas people with a high Classification score pull answers from many different sources all at once. They don't know how they got to an answer; they just got there, and they often do it more quickly than I would. Since my Classification score is low, making quick on-the-spot decisions and working in chaotic work situations is stressful for me and best avoided.

- My *Concept Organization* score: High.
  Concept Organization is the opposite problem-solving style from Classification. Rather than pulling answers from everywhere like Classification, Concept Organization takes information one step at a time and lines it up to reach a conclusion. I am able to arrange ideas easily into a logical sequence and consequently make ideas clear to others. I use this ability any time I'm presenting ideas to another person, planning, or writing, so there will be lots of opportunities for me to use this ability both at work and outside of work.

Don't Waste Your Talent contains a shorthand version of Highlands that is a self-test that you can use to uncover your talents. Or, if you want to go for the full version, which I highly recommend, you can get more details online at **www.highlandsco.com**. The full version is an objective testing system you can take online, on paper, or using a CD-ROM. You'll get an extensive report and individual feedback from a Highlands counselor.

2. **The storytelling way.** Remember those essays you wrote in grade school on the subject of "What I Did This Summer"? It's time to revisit that approach and unearth your talents. Nella Barkley and Eric Sandburg describe these "Life Stories" in their book *The Crystal-Barkley Guide to Taking Charge of Your Career* as "vignettes of happy, rewarding, or meaningful moments that stand out in your mind."[3]

Write two or three short (one to two page) essays about your professional triumphs. For example, write "How I Triumphed Over the Boss from Hell," or "Document Review Guru." Don't limit yourself to your legal career. If you had a previous career, summer jobs, or internships, dredge up those triumphs from your memory banks.

The stories don't have to be just about work. They could be personal triumphs, such as "My College A Cappella Group's Meteoric Rise to Stardom," or "How I Created the Blood Bank Drive of the Century." Think about volunteer opportunities you've taken advantage of, extracurricular activities, or family events you've planned, like your parents' surprise fiftieth wedding anniversary party.

Or consider academic achievements that you are especially proud of, from "How I Scored the Leading Role in the Law School Parody" to "Queen of the Environmental Law Journal." Again, these essays don't have to be related to your life in the legal field. Go back to college or even high school. Like, "How I Talked My Way into Princeton," or "The Thesis of the Century."

Select essay topics that have a story line—a beginning, a middle, and an end. Choose something with a lot of challenges and describe how you overcame them. Let me give you an outline of a good story.

The Frog Becomes a Rowing Prince

Freshman year of college I saw a crew match and fell in love with rowing, but the evil coach wasn't interested in me joining the team because I'd never rowed before. I trained for weeks on end and met all of the coach's impossible tasks. The coach asked me to join the rowing team second semester, and the rest of the team lifted me on their collective shoulders and threw me into the river. The team and I lived happily ever after.

According to *The Crystal-Barkley Guide to Taking Charge of Your Career*,

> One important reward of telling your life stories is that as you recall incidents from your past, forgotten [talents] and strengths emerge and you begin to see yourself in a fresh light. Many of us find it surprising to realize that we can capitalize on [talents] that came naturally to us as children. The trouble is that many of these [talents] fall into disuse because we lose touch with them while doing jobs that use lesser strengths. [R]ecognizing our natural [talents] has a lot to do with knowing how to create rewarding work.[4]

After you've written your essays, read each one separately and write down every single talent you see reflected in the essay. Be creative here. Just because "Coming into the middle of a messy situation, figuring out the issues, and cleaning it up quickly" isn't a skill you'd find on any list doesn't make it invalid. Don't use one-word descriptors, like "Researching," because they don't tell you anything. Write down something more descriptive, like "Learning everything I can about a topic that appeals to me (by going online, reading every book I can find, interviewing others), and condensing it so that I can explain it to others well." These types of talents are where the juice is going to be for you.

If you've provided enough detail in your essays, you should be able to identify at least five to ten talents from each one. Once you've extracted the talents from one essay, move on to the next until you've created a list of talents from each one. What you're doing is uncovering your *natural abilities*, which are talents that you enjoy using, rather than just skills that you are good at.

Once you have a rich list of talents, sort them by grouping similar talents into categories. Then, come up with a descriptive name for each category.

When I wrote my life stories, I came up with the following.

- Easily and enthusiastically motivating myself and others using visualization and curiosity.

- Seeking and finding satisfaction in daydreaming, self-improvement, and beauty.

- Willingly taking on the challenge of revitalizing traditional programs and self by incorporating new ideas.

When I read over my talent categories, I almost wept because I wanted to use these talents so desperately. And, surprise, surprise, it describes the work I'm doing today.

If you want to use this approach to identify your talents, I strongly recommend that you take a look at *The Crystal-Barkley Guide to Taking Charge of Your Career*, as the book contains detailed instructions on how to write life stories and extract your talents from them.

You can use assessments or storytelling to unearth your talents. For extra credit, do both. I found them both to be incredibly insightful—the Highlands Ability Battery provided objective confirmation of what I suspected might be my talents, and telling life stories served as a way of creating rich, detailed examples that brought my talents to life.

WHAT CAREER POSSIBILITIES EXCITE YOU, OTHER THAN TAKING A SABBATICAL?

Gather together a group of three to five trusty friends to help you brainstorm career possibilities. You can include family members if you like, but only if they're supportive. Children are fantastic brainstormers, by the way.

Brainstorming Guidelines

Write your ideas down. Have your notebook handy and ask one of your friends to jot down all the ideas that come out of the session. (This is to keep you from censoring any of the ideas.)

Absolutely no evaluating. Whether you like an idea or don't like it, think it's feasible or ridiculous, it doesn't matter. Just say, "Thank you."

All ideas are welcome. Tell your friends you want *all* their ideas—no matter how silly or impractical they think they are. Emphasize that there is no evaluation allowed. You want a free flow of ideas. If someone throws something out and you say, "I could never do that," it chills participation, and you may miss out on a career possibility that fascinates you. Choose someone to zap anyone who tries to critique. This role is good for your bossy friend.

Brainstorming Session Steps

1. Read your ideal day to the group.

2. Ask, "What career possibilities come to mind?" Have a friend write them down. Remember, neither you nor anyone else should evaluate the ideas. Just write them down. You should be throwing out ideas as well, no matter how wild and crazy you think they are.

3. Share your interest categories and a sample of the interests listed in each category.

4. Ask, "What career possibilities come to mind?" Have your friends write them down.

5. Share your talent categories with the group.

6. Again, ask, "What career possibilities come to mind?" Have your friends write these down, too.

7. Thank your friends and send them home.

8. Close your notebook and go do something else. I mean it. No evaluating, no analyzing, no contemplating. Watch TV, read that juicy brainless novel, or take a nap.

Which Career Possibilities Excite You?

Give yourself a few days, then come back. Pull out your notes from the brainstorming session and take a look. What options appeal to you? Again, this isn't about analyzing whether they are feasible or not. It's strictly about asking yourself what you want to explore.

Make a list of three to five career possibilities you want to explore. And if you've thought of something you want to explore that didn't come up in the exercises or brainstorming, by all means, add it. It's your list.

YOU DID IT!

Congratulations! You put your complaining behind you (or at least to the side) and brainstormed some exciting career possibilities. What courage and heart you've shown. Savor this moment.

And don't try to act like it's not a big deal. For my face-to-face clients, it's like starting an exercise program. You work hard and even lose some weight, but your eyes trick you into thinking that nothing has changed. Your mind may try to do the same thing to you here. Just look back at all your notes to see what you've accomplished. There's your proof.

Need more proof? Talk to one of those unhappy lawyers who didn't come along on this quest with you. I bet they're still complaining about how they have no idea what they want to do. Pity them. Or tell them to buy a copy of this book.

APPRECIATE UNCERTAINTY

You're excited about the possibilities you've come up with. Then all of a sudden it hits you that you don't have anything concrete—no clear idea of what you want to do or a plan for how to get there if you did.

Uncomfortable, isn't it? For most of your working life, you've known what you wanted to do—become a lawyer. So you took the LSAT, applied to law school, earned your JD, interviewed at law firms, and passed the bar exam. Now that you've discovered you want to take a different route and don't have that same clarity, you're frustrated.

You'd give anything for certainty. But I'm going to urge you to do something counterintuitive—appreciate the uncertainty.

Welcome uncertainty because it's actually a place of rich creativity and possibility. One week of feeling uncertain is going to feel like an eternity. And yet it may take several months or more before you gain some clarity.

I promise you that if you're willing to sit with the uncertainty, you will eventually emerge with a sense of direction, a sense of purpose. You may not be able to create the same cookie-cutter plan that exists for becoming a lawyer, but you will have enough to help you take the first step. And what you learn from that first step will guide you to the second step and the next one and the next one.

HARD TRUTH

With each chapter, I'll share a "Hard Truth." A "Hard Truth" is your reality check. It's when I point out where I see you making excuses, avoiding the obvious, and standing in the way of your dreams. It's not always pretty, but it's what I see. I wouldn't be doing my job as a coach if I didn't challenge you when you're not furthering your agenda— which, if you picked up this book, is finding work you love and getting out of the practice of law.

Ready for a Hard Truth, then? Here goes:

It's tempting to want to figure all of this out quickly and leap. Don't. How many lawyers do you know read a job posting, interview, and start their new job only to find themselves miserable again in a few months or years? Better to spend some time figuring this out and exploring the possibilities.

Since I know you're a skeptical bunch, I'm making the assumption that you won't always trust what I'm telling you. So I'll include a case study about a lawyer-turned-"X" who proves my point. Just because I've left the law doesn't mean I don't still understand the value of case law.

CASE STUDY
• • • • • • • • • • •

Debbie Goldstein, age 32
Managing Director, Triad Consulting Group, Cambridge, Mass.
4 years in conflict resolution consulting and training
BA in History/Williams College
JD/Boston College Law School
Years of practice: 0

There's a tremendous amount of pressure in law school to practice for at least a few years. I remember watching in astonishment as a law school professor berated a friend of mine because she'd decided to pursue an alternative route straight out of law school rather than practice law. I think it takes a special kind of courage to go to law school and then not practice law at all.

Debbie is one woman who did just that. She has always lived by her own definition of success and has done just fine.

Describe what you do.

I'm a consultant specializing in conflict resolution. That really encompasses many things. I teach negotiation and communication content, specializing in Difficult Conversation[5] content. I also do mediation and facilitation. I do a bit of writing, as well as teaching at law schools and medical schools.

Let's make the readers jealous and tell them about all of the fascinating work that you do and the neat places you travel.

I worked in Cyprus with public policy students from all over the world, teaching them conflict resolution skills and how to facilitate conversations amongst themselves, as they were a really diverse group. I worked with the Ethiopian Parliament to help its members develop their negotiation skills. I've been to South Africa to assist the country's largest banking group in continuing to make strides with respect to diversity.

I've also gotten to do lots of great work with Fortune 100 countries and given speeches all over the United States—everywhere from Los Angeles to San Francisco to Seattle, New York, Chicago, and Atlanta. I traverse the country on a regular basis.

How did you end up being a conflict resolution consultant?

I came to law school by default. In college I was pre-med. When I realized my organic chemistry class was going to be the death of me, I dropped pre-med. I really didn't know what to do. So of course I went to law school.

At law school I realized pretty early on that "one of these things is not like the other"[6]—everyone was talking about corporate law jobs, summer clerkships, making all this money—and it just filled me with dread. It was just not for me in any sense.

And I found practicing law [based on summer clerkship positions and a stint as a paralegal before law school] really boring. I didn't find it interesting. I didn't find that I was excited to do it. I enjoyed law school; it was intellectually stimulating. But not practicing.

And then I took a mediation course. That was a huge light bulb moment when I realized that there was something I could do that would make me feel really good about using my law degree. Mediation specifically, but more broadly, conflict resolution.

To pursue an alternative job, the experts tell you to network, so that's what I did. I hated it. I knocked on doors, called alumni who were mediators. They all said, "That's great you have an interest, but mediation doesn't have a career path. The only way you're going to get into it is to be a lawyer, find a niche, and pray." I was actually really discouraged about it.

Then one night I was at my brother's house, lamenting that I'd found this wonderful field that excited me and that I was never going to get to do it because it's impossible to get a job in it. My brother told me he thought there was a mother at his daughter's school who did exactly what I was talking about. He said her name was Sheila Heen. My jaw just dropped. I'd read *Difficult Conversations* [*Sheila is a coauthor of the book*].

I said, "Do you think she'd talk to me? Obviously she would never give me a job, but would she just talk to me so I could have more information about the field?" My brother said, "Sure, she's from Nebraska; if you just bring her a bagel, I'm sure she'd be happy to talk to you." My sister-in-law contacted Sheila, who said that she'd be happy to meet with me to give me the lay of the land, but cautioned that she couldn't offer me a job. Apparently, people were always asking her for a job.

Sheila and I met three months later (we had a time getting our schedules coordinated) at 10:00 a.m. at a bagel place (of course) in Cambridge. Our meeting was only supposed to be for half an hour. Sheila had made that clear before we met. She was quite apologetic but had a very busy schedule that day.

We started talking, and when we finally stopped and looked at our watches, it was three hours later! She offered me a job on the spot. She asked if I would be interested in working for her company as I was finishing up law school (I had one more semester) and said that if things worked out, there might be a place for me. Of course I accepted!

I came in as the office manager. I was basically like a secretary. It was all administrative work. I had to really swallow my pride because my friends in law school were going into law firms making $100,000, and I was making $30,000 as my starting salary. [*Debbie now makes in the six figures.*] I really looked at it as a medical student would look at a residency.

It was the best decision I ever made.

After three months in administration, I started doing double duty and took on some consulting work. I showed them I was willing to do anything and everything. That turned out to be instrumental in them bringing me into the company, pretty much folding me into the company in perpetuity. I was working crazy hours. I became a full-time consultant after about a year.

What fears did you have about not becoming a practicing lawyer?

There is a lot of social pressure. It felt a little bit like I was failing by not doing the whole corporate law thing. There was a weird part of me that worried I was failing and worried that other people looked at me and thought I was failing.

That was pretty short-lived, though, because I've always done what feels right anyway, but there was that little voice in my head that had that fear.

I was also worried what my family would think. I could hear them saying, "You went to law school and you're gonna be what? A secretary? What?!" Actually, my family has always been very supportive. But I didn't go into this job saying, "I'm going to be a secretary and who knows." My intention was, "I'm going to be an office manager, and I'm definitely going to move up." I knew the role was going to change.

I was also definitely having financial worries. I knew I couldn't live in Boston on $30,000. I was fortunate in that my parents gave me a loan.

Define success.

Success for me is just so simple. It's, are you happy? Do you feel like you're making a contribution to society? Do you wake up feeling good about what you do and who's in your life? Nothing more than that.

How did you know conflict resolution was the career for you?

It really was an "aha" moment. The reason why I wanted to go into medicine in the first place is that it's my nature to help people. I always want to be the person someone talks to, confides in, and seeks advice from. I'm the person who sits next to a stranger on the bus and by the time we get to her destination she has told me everything about herself.

Then I went into law, and it didn't feel like I was helping people or myself. It felt adversarial. But when I discovered mediation, it felt like the perfect marriage of helping people and using the law degree that I'd wasted three years to get.

It felt as natural as the sky is blue.

What makes you different from lawyers who don't pursue their dreams?

A big part of it is I'm so lucky that I didn't have the financial push that I had to go get a $120,000-a-year job coming out of law school. [*Debbie's parents paid for her college and law school education.*] I didn't have debt to pay, so I had the luxury of being able to do what I wanted. I can't deny that was a piece of it.

Another definite piece is that the definition of success in my family has always been what makes you happy. Being successful isn't "Debbie working in a firm being miserable." It's "Debbie doing what she loves to do." There was no pressure to do what might look good so that my parents could brag about me to their friends at dinner parties. My parents define success as what makes you happy—following your heart. It wasn't such a hard decision because of that.

There's a story Sheila [*Debbie's boss*] tells that I think is relevant to the question you asked about why some people stay in a job that makes them miserable. One of Sheila's friends had a baby. The baby was two years old and needed a diaper change. The kid didn't want to have his diaper changed. His mom insisted, "Yes, we have to change you. You pooped." The kid was adamant. "No, I don't want to." His mom finally asked, "Why?" The kid explained, "Because it's cozy."

Some people are cozy with what they do even if they're sitting in [crap]. You get comfortable with where you are even if you're sitting in misery.

What pressures did you experience to go the traditional route?

I felt a lot of pressure because there were zero other options than the corporate firm at the career counseling office. I was the only person I knew in law school who didn't go the typical lawyer route.

What's the purpose of work in your life?

I spend so much time at work—it's like a home for me, an extension of who I am. Part of why I love what I do is the people I work with.

My whole life is relationship-focused. Having the job I do allows me to be relationship-focused.

I love my job in every aspect—well, except last week when a client called while I was on vacation. One minute I was on vacation and the next minute, I was on a conference call every day, and that was not fun.

Anything else you want to share?

Life's too short to practice law if you don't want to. You don't get any prize for wallowing in your misery. At the end of your life, you don't get rewarded for that.

● ● ● ● ● ● ● ● ● ● ● ●

WHAT YOU SHOULD HAVE LEARNED IN THIS CHAPTER

There are key points in each chapter I want to burn into your brain. Rather than having you guess what they are, I'll include a checklist at the end of each chapter.

☐ Figuring out what you want from your work and life is critical—do not proceed until you figure it out.

☐ While practicing law may have narrowed your vision, you've now busted it wide open because you've discovered you have interests, talents, and a list of exciting career possibilities to explore.

☐ Resist the urge to bolt from your job. Uncertainty can be painful, but it's a crucial part of the process.

☐ Get ready for a roller coaster of an adventure!

chapter two

Ditch Your Friends Who Are Lawyers

LETTER FROM A DESPERATE LAWYER

Dear Monica,

I just found out there's a secret society of lawyers at my firm who hate practicing law. They've invited me to join. They sneak into someone's office to talk about how miserable their lives are. Sounds good to me. What do you think?

Joe

Here's a multiple choice question for you: how do you know when it's time to ditch your lawyer friends?

(a) Their idea of taking action is getting together at happy hour to complain over martinis.

(b) Their idea of brainstorming career possibilities is to send you random legal job postings.

(c) Their idea of finding career satisfaction is to change firms every two years.

(d) All of the above.

This chapter describes the importance of surrounding yourself with people who are creative, who will inspire you, who will challenge you, and who will accept nothing less than your letter of resignation.

WHO ARE YOU SPENDING YOUR TIME WITH?

You know that definition of insanity as doing the same thing over and over again? Well, it's also insane to expect to be able to make a career change if you hang out with the same people over and over again.

Why is that? Just think about the folks you surround yourself with—family, friends, colleagues. How many of these people knew you when you were in law school or once you became a lawyer? How many of them knew you *before* you were a lawyer—a college student, or if law is your second career, in your first career? I'll bet most of these people know you as a lawyer. Folks who know you as a lawyer have a hard time visualizing you as anything else. So here's what you have to do.

Kick Your Friends to the Curb

I'm telling you to get rid of your friends in a tongue-in-cheek manner...sort of. You don't have to get rid of your friends if they're supportive types. But even if they are, you may need to stop relying on them to help you make a career change. Why? Because some of your friends only know you as lawyer you. They don't know you as anyone else and can't imagine you as anyone else.

Have you noticed that when you ask these friends for ideas, they suggest switching firms, practice groups, or going in-house? They don't have a clue what to suggest because in their minds, once you're a lawyer, you're always a lawyer. And why would anyone not want to be a lawyer anyway? Some of them may secretly think that you're going through a quarter-life or mid-life crisis and that if they just humor you, you'll come to your senses.

Not to mention I'm betting a lot of the people you know are lawyers. How many of them are happy practicing law? I can count the happy lawyers I know on one hand. How many of them are successful at finding other opportunities? Expecting these people to help you make a career change is the proverbial blind leading the blind. The miserable blind leading the miserable blind, actually.

It's the rare lawyer I know who wants to make a career change and sees unlimited possibilities for herself. More likely she's spending her time griping about how she doesn't know what she wants to do, doesn't know how she'd get out if she did, and asking you if you have seen the latest legal postings. Not inspirational.

If you simply must hang out with lawyers, hang out with lawyers who are no longer practicing law, who have awesome careers that they love—even if they're not careers you're interested in. Because what you need most right now is some encouragement, some inspiration, and someone who will tell you that the life you want to have is possible.

MAKE SOME NEW FRIENDS

Remember those career possibilities you came up with? It's time to make some friends in those careers—even if you're not sure which career you want to pursue.

This approach serves a dual purpose. First, it helps you to establish an all important lifeline—the lifeline to a world outside of law. These new friends are going to be your links to this strange, new world.

Second, it gives you a chance to test-drive your new career. If you're not so interested in the folks in your new field, you're probably not going to enjoy that field. Case in point—practicing law. How many of your current colleagues are you trying to emulate? Most of my clients are scrambling to find a way not to have the lives their legal colleagues and higher-ups have.

The same principle applies with respect to your new career. For example, I thought I'd be interested in organizational development. So I went to a meeting of my local organizational development society. I didn't meet a single person I was interested in getting to know better. I thought it was possible that none of the cool people came to that meeting, so just to be sure, I went to another meeting. I met a few potentially interesting folks. So I made coffee or lunch plans with them and "auditioned" them. My intuition told me the same thing—not my people.

On the other hand, when I explored coaching, I met a lot of kindred spirits. I developed new friendships and, most importantly, began to see myself as a part of the group. I began, albeit very slowly, to see myself as maybe one day becoming a coach.

The other great thing about connecting with your new world is that you will make new friends who will push you off the cliff of indecision into your new world, whether you think you're ready or not. An instructor at a coaching class told me I was a natural and insisted I sign up for the rest of the class series. Another friend insisted I take on my first client. Another forced me to send out an announcement about my coaching business. These new friends are vital to you making a career change.

A Quick Primer on Making New Friends

Some folks are natural-born socializers. They move to a new town and, before you know it, half the town is going to dinner at their house. If meeting new people is as easy as breathing to you, don't scratch your head and wonder why I'm explaining how to do this; just skip this section.

For the rest of us, this skill may be pretty rusty. One client described the issue as follows: "I haven't had to make new friends in years. It's easy to fall into a rut. After all, I have a pretty limited calendar—to work, home, and back again. Occasionally the gym, errands, maybe a few social activities. But it's always with the same people. I haven't had a reason to try to meet anyone new. So how do you do that again?"

It's no wonder meeting new people is a challenge. It's easy in college and law school. There's a whole group of people thrown together in new circumstances who are there to meet new people. That happens to some extent when you start a new job, but after that, good luck.

The way to meet new people is to break your routine. I'm not asking you to turn your whole schedule upside down. You just need to add a few new activities, preferably an activity related to one of the career possibilities you're exploring. Let's say you're interested in becoming a potter, having your own store, and selling your pottery and others' work. You could sign up for an eight-week pottery class at your local arts institute.

Trying to make new friends might feel a bit awkward at first. It's not like you can just walk up to someone and say, "Hi, let's be friends." That tends to scare people if you're past the age of 8. What you could do is just make sure to meet everyone in the class and engage in inconsequential chitchat for the first few weeks. Once you meet someone you think you might like to get to know better, invite him or her to coffee or a field trip to a pottery store.

When I took my pottery class, part of the homework was to come back as often as possible to practice. You could schedule a play date with one of your classmates. There's lots of time to talk and laugh when you're screwing up making bowls on the wheel.

The key is to break out of your routine and try some new activities—and to keep your eyes open while you're doing them. We're used to walking around with blinders on when it comes to meeting new people because we think we don't need (or have time for) any new friends. That's changed now. What you need most are new friends with fresh ideas, different ways of looking at things, and spontaneity. New friends who see you as you are now—a lawyer looking for a new career.

QUICK TIP

Quickest way to make new friends? Join something. Interested in the arts? Join an arts organization that puts on an annual festival. There's nothing like working in the trenches on a project to build relationships fast.

SUPPORT GROUP

You need more than new friends. Heck, leaving the law can feel like such a Herculean task, you need a support group. Yes, yes, I know you're perfectly capable of tackling all challenges single-handedly. Lawyers as a general rule abhor asking anyone for help. We are self-sufficient, thank you very much.

Not when it comes to changing careers, though. You cannot do it alone. I've had so many clients tell me that they didn't come to me at first because they were sure that they and their brilliant intellect could solve this career problem on their own. Months (or years) later when they still hadn't done anything, they had to admit they needed help. That's when they called me.

The trick is to find a way to surround yourself consistently and systematically with supportive people who can show you what's right about you, or dare I say, what's genius about you. You need a support group.

What's the advantage of working with a support group? So many things! Lawyers who are unhappy often feel so alone. If you're sitting in a room with six other lawyers who feel the same way, you finally get validation that the way you're feeling isn't so wacky or unusual. You get the emotional support you need.

It's also easy to develop tunnel vision when you're on this trek by yourself. With others in the room, you have several sources of ideas, different perspectives, creative approaches, lessons learned, resources, and brainstorming. Additionally, you have accountability, cheerleading when you're making progress, and a kind push when you're hiding. Most importantly, there's something about a group like this that builds momentum. On your own this journey can take forever, but you can cut years off the process by working with others.

Why Some Groups Work and Others Bomb

If you've had a less-than-stellar group experience in the past, don't just skip over this section. I used to feel lackluster about the concept of support groups, too. I'd been involved with some groups that just didn't work. I didn't get anything out of the experience, or we got together and didn't get anything done, or we just stopped getting together. We often started with big dreams and lots of excitement, but for some reason it just fizzled.

The groups don't work if there's too much or too little structure. Manage this balance by doing your planning up front, set the thing up, and then let it run. Here are some tips.

Select your members carefully. Start the group by inviting two or three people you think would make good group members. I'm a fan of motivated, upbeat self-starters who are compassionate and good at brainstorming. Then you and the other group founders can decide on the criteria for who else you'll invite. The group isn't just for any lawyer who's unhappy. You're looking for folks who are committed to making a change and committed to helping each other do the same.

Keep the size manageable—no more than ten people. If you can, try to get at least seven or eight people because if there are only four or five of you and one gets pregnant and drops out, one thinks it's too hard and gives up, and another moves because her spouse gets a job in another city, it's just you and one other person staring at each other. If there are only three or four of you, check out the section on the buddy system.

You don't all have to be in the same place in the game. One of you can know what alternative career you want to pursue, another can have no clue, and one can be in the process of making the transition. The only place you all need to be is a place where you are fired up to get out of the law and into what fits you.

Set a schedule in advance. Don't get sloppy about this and say, "Oh, I'm sure we'll get together whenever we can." Decide on a schedule for the duration of the group meetings at the beginning. It is a challenge coordinating eight schedules, so you want to get this taken care of up front. If you're open to the possibility, you could even meet over the telephone. This eliminates traffic challenges, setting a meeting place, etc. There are lots of free conference call services available, some that will even let you record your calls. Some folks much prefer meeting in person, so you may have to negotiate this issue.

Set a limit on the number of sessions (and the duration of the sessions) in advance. People need a finite time in which to accomplish goals. If left open-ended, you could take the rest of your life to leave the law. For example, you could meet once a month for ninth months for two hours each meeting.

Make sure the members understand and agree to the purpose of the group up front. Meandering, pointless get-togethers are best left for law firm meetings. Be clear about your purpose for this group at the beginning. It's not a social gathering. It's not a vent session. It's not a gossip session. You are here for the purpose of supporting each other in making a career transition. Get each member to verbally commit to the purpose and to agree to remind each other of that as you go forward.

Create a loose structure for your meetings. Notice I used the word *loose*. A printout of an agenda with starting and ending times for each topic will annoy members who like a little more spontaneity. You could start by checking in on successes and failures. Brainstorm and share resources and ideas when there are challenges and celebrate successes, the little ones and the big ones. Create a series of exercises you can do together. Have each member come up with homework to do in between the sessions.

Warning

As tempting as it is to schedule a meeting over a meal, I do not recommend it. Even if it's a potluck at someone's house, most of your time will be taken up by fixing plates, eating, and cleaning up. It's too distracting. There is nothing wrong with a food-laden party when the support group comes to an end to celebrate your successes, though.

Be a coach. Select a person—preferably someone different each time—to facilitate each meeting. Sure, it would be great to have a trained coach in the room, but you can learn how to coach each other. Coaching is about being curious. It's about championing each other and challenging each other. Ask open-ended questions. Make sure everyone in the group (including you) gets the opportunity to speak. Notice if someone is stuck and needs brainstorming, an opportunity to vent, or an acknowledgment.

Take advantage of the power of working together. There is magic in camaraderie. Open up to your group and be prepared to be amazed at what you can accomplish when you have support.

THE BUDDY SYSTEM

Remember the *buddy system* in grade school? You took a field trip to a museum and you had to stay with your buddy at all times. Right about now, you could really use a buddy on this field trip of career exploration. All right, in truth, this person doesn't necessarily have to be a buddy. What you're really looking for is someone who will make a commitment to partner with you on your journey from practicing lawyer to nonpracticing happy person.

Partner Up...But Choose Wisely

You're working on something major here. So don't pick a good friend just because she's a good friend. Is this the friend who has trouble keeping track of her calendar or who enjoys being the voice of doom and gloom? If so, she's not a good choice. What you're looking for is someone who wants to make a big change in her life. And it doesn't necessarily have to be a lawyer making a career change or even a nonlawyer making a career change. It could be someone who has a dream of racing dogs at the Iditarod Trail Sled Dog Race, for example. You want someone who is as committed to making this change as you are.

If there's more than two of you, you can still partner up, but you'll use a *round robin approach*. Let's say Alice, Sharon, and Mark want to start a support group, but think their group is a bit small, so they decide to partner up instead. As a group, they select one person in the group to be another person's coach. Alice selects Sharon to be her coach, Sharon selects Mark to be her coach, and Mark selects Alice to be his coach.

Give the Relationship Some Structure

Just like the support group has structure, this partnership needs structure. Otherwise, it's too easy for your time together to devolve into a gab fest or a vent session. Each pair can schedule separate coaching times: coach each other thirty minutes every week or sixty minutes every other week for three months. Start the session by discussing successes and failures, get coaching on a challenge, and set homework. Like the support group, you can coach over the telephone or schedule in-person sessions.

Get to Know Your Partner Up Front

I'm not talking about asking what her astrological sign or favorite dessert is. Since you're working one-on-one, you can design a relationship that capitalizes on your strengths and bolsters your weaknesses. Interview your partner and ask the following six questions.[7]

1. What do you want to accomplish? If you had to describe yourself as moving from Point A to Point B, what are Points A and B?

2. What works when you're successful at making changes?

3. Where do you usually get stuck?

4. What motivates you when you're stuck?

5. How do you deal with disappointment or failure?

6. How are you about doing what you say you'll do?

You're gathering information that is going to be incredibly useful. Once you understand what makes your partner tick, you can find ways to keep her motivated and know what to do when she falls down. You can remind your partner of her tendency to get caught up in the small details instead of focusing on the big picture, or you can give your partner space to have a temper tantrum if that's how she deals with disappointment. And obviously, your partner can do the same for you.

Let me show you how this might look. Recently I was lamenting my inability to eat any food that has any nutritional value. I decided I was going to do something about it. Usually I just launch into my campaign of self-improvement and a few weeks later (sometimes only days later), I'm back to my old habits. I thought, "Well, you're a coach; use some of those fancy skills you acquired." So I interviewed myself using the six questions previously listed and came up with the following answers.

1. Point A is food with no nutritional value; headachey, worn out. Point B is healthy eating (but the food has to taste good), increased energy, and feeling good.

2. What works when I'm successful at making changes is a push, a plan, baby steps, visualizing the idea, and being accountable to someone.

3. I usually get stuck when I have too many goals and have to prioritize, it's too big/complex of a plan, there are too many details, new goals pop up and distract me, and it feels overwhelming/too hard.

4. What motivates me when I'm stuck is a plan, a vision, remembering the benefits, and a push.

5. I don't deal with disappointment or failure well at all. I get down on myself, berate myself. I tend to do the opposite of the behavior I'm trying to do. I cry.

6. I'm not so good about doing what I say I'll do. I'm a big dreamer but not so good at follow-through. When I feel accountable, then I'm eager to please. I probably need a partner.

I thought carefully about who I wanted to work with (she's a fellow coach), contacted her to see if she had any big changes she wanted to make (she did), and we got this partnership going.

Thanks to my partner, with whom I shared my answers, instead of my usual approach, which is a complex battle plan featuring the cold turkey method, I'm simply introducing myself to one new healthy food (that tastes good) a week and enjoying the process.

HIRE A COACH

If left to our own devices, we lawyers will analyze and agonize and take very little action. We will get stuck in the miry pit of our fears, doubts, and everyone else's opinions.

A coach helps you climb out of the pit. Whether it's asking tough questions, brainstorming, motivating you, and cheering you on when you triumph, or picking you up when you stumble, a coach is your champion.

A coach also focuses solely on your agenda. While family and friends may have your best interests at heart, they often confuse *their* interests with yours. It's so refreshing to work with someone who only wants what you want and will help you remember what that is when you get confused.

HARD TRUTH

It's a weird thing. Even what makes us miserable can be comfortable. I call it the *old shoe theory*. Old shoes are usually pretty raggedy—scuff marks, maybe some holes are beginning to form in the soles—but they're also really comfortable. So it's hard to give them up. Like your friends. It's comfortable to go to happy hour with your buddies from work and gripe about your careers. But meanwhile, nothing's changing and time is going by. Is this really what you want?

Take a good, hard look at who you spend your time with. If these people aren't giving you the support, encouragement, ideas, and push you need, it's time to step out of your comfort zone and find people who will.

CASE STUDY
• • • • • • • • • • • •

Voltaire Sterling, age 27
Stage and Screen Actor, Producer, Philanthropist; Beverly Hills, Calif.
9 months in film and theater
BA in Business Administration, Concentration: Marketing;
  Minor: Spanish/Morehouse College, semester abroad at the University of
  Granada, Spain
JD/Harvard Law School
Years of practice: 1
Type of practice: corporate, mid-sized firm in Los Angeles, Calif.

Voltaire is a shining example of someone who knows the value of surrounding himself with people who are supportive (and protecting himself from those who aren't). Granted, he is fortunate because he has a family who encourages him to follow his dreams. But there's so much more to it than that. During our interview, Voltaire mentioned countless times the people who he met, who he talked to, who he pursued, who he built a relationship with, and who mentored him.

Voltaire has a special talent for building relationships not only with supportive people, but also with powerful people with the ability to help him. I realize we don't all have this talent, but you can cultivate some of the skills that he has—going after the people you want to meet, being persistent, asking for help, sharing your story with others, helping others, getting involved in lots of different activities and events, and following up with people—heck, sending thank you notes! Sure, he's in an industry where who you know matters enormously, but I submit to you that building relationships is a crucial part of making a career transition, no matter what industry you are trying to break into.

Describe what you do. That seems an odd question to ask an actor. Obviously the answer is, "I act." But I'd love to hear what you think.

I interpret stories and bring them to life either on stage or on screen. At this level of my career I'm doing sales a lot; I'm more than just an actor. I'm my own publicist. I have a manager now, but didn't initially, and I don't have an agent yet, so a lot of what I do is read scripts and stay abreast of what the industry is doing. I have friends who work at different companies. I serve as an advocate for myself.

How did you end up becoming an actor?

I've always loved the arts. Growing up I was always in plays in church, in the community, and school. In college I got together with some of my friends and produced a play, August Wilson's *Joe Turner's Come and Gone*. Shortly after the play closed, August Wilson came to Morehouse to receive an award. I lobbied to present the award to him and we had the opportunity to present a few scenes for him, and he loved it. That was one of my best experiences there.

I knew that ultimately I wanted to work as an actor or an entertainment lawyer because I thought that entertainment law would be close enough to acting that I would still feel fulfilled. Because I had an interest in acting and being creative, and I also like being an advocate, I thought I could advocate on behalf of others if I'm not going to be an artist myself.

[*Voltaire went to Harvard Law School but was torn about practicing law.*] I'd done just legal jobs during the summers. It was never my passion, never the goal I had in mind. I'd just accepted my offer with a firm and it was not exactly what I wanted to do. But you get sucked into this path. And they pay a lot of money.

My 3L year I was a little down, needing some inspiration. I was in church praying, and I had an epiphany. I thought, "I should bring Hill Harper back to Harvard Law and have him talk about his exciting career, his nontraditional path in an effort to inspire my classmates." [*Harper is an actor currently starring in the television show* CSI: NY *and also a graduate of Harvard Law. Voltaire met Harper after seeing him perform in the play* Blue *in New York.*] Really, I was doing it for me because I needed it. I called it the first annual "Live Your Dream" event at Harvard Law School. It was a wonderful, wonderful event. Over 250 people came out and were really inspired.

[*After graduation, Voltaire joined a firm in Los Angeles, California.*] The crazy thing about it was [the firm] was a wonderful opportunity because it showed me if I can't be happy here, then there's no way I can be happy in this profession. They laid out the red carpet for me. It's a fun place to work. The people are really cool. And they do interesting work.

Even amid all that, I was miserable, dying a slow death. I loathed going to the office because there were some days I could just close my door and not see anyone and that was really not the life I'd envisioned for myself.

So I started thinking back to what it was exactly that I wanted to do when I was a kid, before [those] outside voices came in and told me "You can't." It was acting. I also decided I don't want to get to a point where it's too late and say, "I wished I could have."

[*Voltaire left the firm and joined Overbrook Entertainment, the production company co-run by Will Smith, Academy Award–nominated actor and rap artist. He worked as an assistant for one of the executives at the company. He got the job with the help of a friend who introduced him to his future boss.*]

The jump to Overbrook Entertainment was very timely. First jump. Great buffer. Money I was making at the firm was $125,000. To jump from that to making absolutely nothing as an actor would be a horrific jump. I don't know that I would have been able to do it. But God stepped in and presented this opportunity to me. I was making a fifth of what I was making at the firm. But there has never been a day that I have missed working at the firm.

[*However, the job didn't turn out to be what Voltaire expected, and after three months he decided to leave.*] At that point I was scared. I made this jump. It was not a safe move. It was a risky one. And I was in this place that didn't look like it would work out. [The thought crossed my mind that m]aybe I should have just stayed. It was a crisis and I thought, "What am I going to do?"

After I left [Overbrook] I spent a little time in prayer. It was a soul-searching period. I wasn't talking to many people at all. I didn't want to muddle my own thoughts. I was weighing a few different options.

I considered going to work for Harper full-time at his foundation. [*Voltaire had cultivated and built a friendship with Harper after the Harvard Law event.*] I had to talk Harper into thinking about me for the position, actually. He said, "I don't think this is the right move for you," because he knows what my dreams are and what I want to do. And it's easy to get sidetracked just because something is easy. Ultimately, I turned it down and decided to pursue acting.

I went to a play that a friend was performing in at Theater Palisades (a local community theater) and saw that they were going to be doing *A Few Good Men*. I auditioned for a role and got the part. While I was doing the play, I was also taking an acting class. I got wind via class of a film Denzel Washington [*Academy Award–winning actor, director*] was going to be working on called *The Great Debaters*. Denzel is one of my all-time heroes. I went home and looked up the film and saw Denzel was going to be directing. I thought it would be amazing to work for him. Of course it was impossible and nuts for me to be thinking that I could just jump into this and land a role in this man's film.

I started this all-out [mission] thinking about anyone and everyone I could think of who might be able to get me in front of Denzel. I sent my headshot and résumé to everyone I knew.

Mid April I got an email that I'll never forget. It was from the film's casting director and it said, "I got your headshot from Denzel. We would like you to put yourself on tape for a part." I was screaming. [*Voltaire submitted his audition tape with the help of a friend who went to school for film at NYU.*]

The next week I got an email that said, "Great news." That was the subject line. I thought it was going to say, "We want to bring you back in for a callback" but instead it said, "We have decided to cast you."

I had just the night before come from rehearsal at the play and I was kind of depressed thinking, "Am I doing the right thing?" There are some moments where I get like that, some days. "Is this nuts?" There's no set path. No one hands it to you, you have to carve it out for yourself. I get moments where I'm wondering if I'm making the right choices. And then I got this email.

What fears did you have about not practicing law?

It's a huge time commitment of three years of your life. Financially it's a huge investment. Did I waste my time and money? If at some point I decide I want to go back to the practice of law, will that be possible? What will ultimately come of [going to law school]—will it be helpful in the future?

I'm comfortable in knowing that it was very helpful in some sense because I made some of my best friends, who I think ultimately will be great professional contacts in the future. One of them works for the production company for this movie. One of the ways I was able to hear about it was talking to him. I feel like at some point in life when he's huge in the industry and I am, we'll be sitting on a panel at Harvard Law, talking about how you can make your dreams happen and how a year and a half [after graduating] we were working on a feature film.

Even understanding the deals I'll be in a position to make. I'll understand them a different way than if I hadn't had the legal training and also if I hadn't practiced.

How do you define success?

I'm probably still defining it but at this stage of life I define it by having a certain level of happiness. It's like a happiness meter that I like to think about when I make decisions with regard to how I spend my time and life, maybe because I'm very young and in the mind-set of not having been in a position to make money because I've been in school so long. It may be a bit naïve, but my decisions aren't dictated by financial concerns because my family is very supportive of me. So my decisions are more so dictated by, is this going to make me happy? At the end of the day, will I be able to look in the mirror and feel good about myself? Being able to, at this stage, get up and enjoy life. And be happy about each day and where I'm going.

As I start to look toward the future, financially I want to be able to have a family, provide a good life for them. I love traveling so I want to be in a position to travel. But also I always want to be in a position to reach back and help somebody else who's coming up along the way. Last week, for instance, I was doing a recruitment forum for Harvard Law at Morehouse. Clearly I have left the law and I'm not a lawyer, but I do understand the law school admissions process and want to see numbers of [Morehouse grads] who are going to Harvard Law increase. There's something I can do, having gone there and cultivated relationships with folks who are admissions representatives at the school. I want to continue that. And even outside of the law school context, helping with Harper's foundation MANifest Your Destiny, helping young people achieve what their goals are.

How did you know acting was the career for you?

I love it when I'm on stage. Knowing professionally that I could do it, that it was the career for me? I got less than three hours of sleep [*the night before he filmed his scenes in* The Great Debaters] but the whole [next] day I wasn't tired. I was in my element. We did it so many times but I was so excited. I loved every part of it. This is how I think I know that this is what I'm meant to do. I remember at one point I looked up and I saw the sun beaming and I said, "Thank you, God." This is where I need to be.

What makes you different from lawyers who don't pursue their dreams?

Not much, actually. I have friends who are practicing and they're not really happy, but I think it's just that crucial step, maybe just taking a leap, just trying. Perhaps what sets me and anyone else who makes the leap apart is that when we have those moments of doubt, there's someone or something who can step in to say, "No, you can do it and you will do it. I believe in you." For me, it was having a supportive family (my parents and my brother and sister) and girlfriend and faith in God. I feel like I was led to make the move.

What pressures did you experience to go the traditional route?

People project their fears onto you. You have to be careful who you share your dreams with. Some people, because they're afraid and think they can't do it, will tell you, "Nah, you can't do that. How are you going to be an actor? You're a lawyer." You have to just remember that they haven't always known you. "Just because you know me as a lawyer doesn't mean that that's what I am. What I am at this moment doesn't mean that that's what I have always been."

Another thing is that I have a lot of debt from law school, [and have to] think functionally about how ultimately am I going to pay that back. So of course that's a consideration.

And I want to be able to show my parents while they're still here some of the incredible things I've experienced. They've sacrificed a lot for me and my brother and sister. We've seen the world. I've lived in Europe, traveled extensively throughout Europe and the States and the Caribbean. I want them to experience that, to be in a position to provide that for them. At the moment I'm struggling. That's a huge consideration.

Quite naturally, there's also a lot of internal doubt. It's helpful that even when I don't believe in myself, my friends and family believe in me.

What doesn't appeal to you about practicing?

It was very lonely. I'm a people person. I really enjoy collaborating with others. Getting an assignment from a partner could take 5–10 minutes and then I'd shut my door and I wouldn't see anyone for days. I hated the lonely aspect of it.

That's one of the hardest things about this early stage of my career. There are some days where I literally could not see anyone. Unless I make a point of going out, I could go the whole day without seeing anyone. It's similar to the practice of law, but on the flip side I have the notion of knowing that I'm on my path and it could be something really fulfilling.

In that same moment [*filming* The Great Debaters] when I knew that acting was for me, I knew that law was not for me. There wasn't a day at the firm that I experienced like that day.

It was also depressing to live in a city that's beautiful all the time and to go for a day without being outside. I live in an apartment with underground parking so I could get into my car, drive right into the parking deck at the office, stay in the office all day, come back home, and [it would be] dark already.

What's the purpose of work in your life?

I clearly want to be in a position to affect change. It's not just that I work to live, but to a certain extent I will live to work. Some of the things I want to do will be all-encompassing. I do think work does become definitive of you and what you stand for and who you are, but I want to be in a position to enjoy life. It shouldn't be that there's nothing else that drives me other than pursuing this project or this film and not having any time for loved ones or friends. That's a really important part of my life.

Living in Spain taught me this. In Spain they work because they have to, but they really enjoy life. It's nothing for people to take some time to have a coffee at a café and sit down and catch up. Those slower moments, spending time with people—I love it about the country.

Anything else you want to share?

When I jumped into acting, I had this moment. It's literally a couple of seconds, but it seems like you step outside of yourself and you see the scene play out. A week after I left the firm, I went back to Morehouse to do some recruiting for Harvard Law, but stayed for another event because my mentor, Ingrid Saunders Jones, was there. [*Saunders Jones is the director of corporate external affairs and senior vice president of The Coca-Cola Company, and chairperson of The Coca-Cola Foundation.*] I didn't know what I was doing with my life. Dr. Michael Lomax [*president of the United Negro College Fund*] was sitting at my table. I'd met him before and I went over to say hello. He asked me, "What are you up to these days?" I said, "Well," and I had this moment, "Should I tell him that I'm a lawyer?" I'd just told my mentor the night before, and she'd been very supportive. It was probably only two seconds but I had all of this going on in my head. And I said, "You know what, after law school, I worked at a firm for a while and decided it wasn't for me. And I've now decided to pursue my passion for acting." He said, "You know what's exciting about you telling me that, I might have something of interest. So give me a call." And then he tells my girlfriend, who was with me, "I want him to call me because I might have an additional ticket to the Academy Awards and I want him to go with me." I went to the Oscars this year. I met Lou Gossett, Jr. [*Academy Award–winning actor*] whom I've since kept in touch with and he wants me to be a part of his team for his foundation.

It taught me that we should be courageous. I took that chance [*telling Dr. Lomax that he was no longer practicing law and was pursuing acting*] and Dr. Lomax took me to the Oscars. If I'd said, "I'm a lawyer," that would have been the end of the conversation. It would have gone in a totally different direction.

[*Voltaire also saw Joe Roth, a producer for* The Great Debaters, *at the Oscars.*] I met Joe when he came to Harvard Business School [*while Voltaire was in law school*] and I got wind of the presentation and went over to meet him. At the Oscars, I see this guy looking for a seat and it was Joe Roth. I'd just seen him that week at this event for Barack Obama. [*Voltaire was involved in Obama's presidential campaign.*] When I saw Joe at Obama's event, I reminded him we'd met at Harvard. When I saw him again at the Oscars, we spoke but I didn't know at the time he was going to be producing *The Great Debaters.* After the Oscars I sent him a note, telling him, "It was good to see you, would love to keep in touch." When I found out he was producing the movie, you better believe he was one of the people I sent my headshot and résumé to, saying, "So good to meet you."

On my business card (and this is before all this stuff happened because of my relationship with Harper and I figured out what I wanted to do with my life) it says, "Actor, producer, philanthropist." I'm helping with Harper's foundation, the acting, I produced a play in the past and want to get more into that. But I say that to say, God is really good. He's put these different experiences into my life.

I don't believe in luck. I believe in Providence; our steps are divinely guided. If this whole experience in my life is not an indication of that, I don't know what is.

• • • • • • • • • • • •

WHAT YOU SHOULD HAVE LEARNED IN THIS CHAPTER

☐ Stop trying to force your family and friends to come up with your new career path, because it's highly unlikely they will.

☐ Stop hanging out with lawyers, unless you want to keep reading legal postings for new jobs.

☐ Stop trying to go it alone, unless you want to continue practicing law.

☐ There's a wonderful world out there just waiting to help you, support you, and believe in you.

chapter three

How Can You Explore Possibilities, Other Than Daydreaming about Them?

LETTER FROM A DESPERATE LAWYER

Dear Monica,

As much as I would like to, I just can't leave my job. What if something sounds great and I leave to go do it and I hate it? There has to be some way you can see what other careers are like without actually giving up your job. I don't have summers off so an internship is out. Isn't it?

Andrew

It's time to take action. Already?! Yes, already. I'm not suggesting you turn in your resignation letter tomorrow, but again, this book is not about dreaming about leaving the law—it's about leaving the law.

It's so easy to get stuck in fantasy land. You daydream about getting the job of your dreams and every day is like a Disney film—Technicolor blue sky, and birds land on your finger and whistle a tune. Earth to Dreamer, let's see what the reality is like. It may not be a Disney movie, but it could be everything you ever dreamed of.

EXPLORING THE POSSIBILITIES

I have a very simple exercise you can use to brainstorm ideas for exploring the career possibilities that intrigue you.

Note: You'll need at least one buddy for this exercise, although two would be better.

Remember the brainstorming rules I laid out in the section on "What Career Possibilities Excite You?" The same rules apply here—write down every idea, no evaluating, and tell your brainstorming partners you want every idea they come up with, no censorship.

1. Select the career possibility you want to explore first. Ask your buddies to help you brainstorm ways to explore the career possibility. Again, no evaluation. Just jot down any ideas that come to mind.

2. Select the next career possibility you want to explore. Brainstorm ways you can explore this career option.

3. Continue until you have come up with ways to explore each career possibility.

It doesn't get any easier than that. I also have a few tips to get your mind humming.

CAREER EXPLORATION TIPS

Research

Put those research skills you've honed practicing law to good use. Start by going online. If you're not a whiz at tracking down information on the Internet, find someone who is to help you. You can find articles, official sites, blogs, listservs, book excerpts (and sometimes the whole book), and interviews. There's a wealth of information there. Don't just look for the official stuff. Skim everything you can find, even the stuff written by people whose sanity you question. You'll be surprised what you can learn from the disgruntled.

QUICK TIP

Keep notes of URLs. I can't tell you the number of times I wanted to find a link later but couldn't remember what search I used to get to it. Once that happened a number of times, I got smart and made a practice of copying and pasting URLs with a brief description into a Microsoft Word document.

Next, hit your local bookstores and libraries. The career sections at my local bookstores are jammed full of standard and not-so-standard career guides. If you found some published books online that aren't at your bookstore, a bookstore associate will be happy to order them for you. And, of course, depending upon how good your library is, you may find some resources there, as well. Set aside a few hours, take a notebook, pick up a stack, and settle in.

Sample

I love this approach because you can design it so that it's only a short-term commitment. There's no need to quit your job. Lawyers constantly gripe about how hard it is to explore something without leaving their day job. Not so. Look around for these short-term opportunities because they are everywhere. The following are a few quick ideas to get your brain buzzing.

- Interested in film? Volunteer for your city's film festival organization.

- Think you'd like event planning? Offer to plan a friend's wedding.

- Curious about floral design? Do a *mini-apprenticeship* (spend a day) with a florist.

- Want to race dirt bikes? Take a class.

I can't stress enough how revealing sampling can be. Just think about when you started your law firm job. How long did it take for you to decide this job wasn't it? Three months? A couple of weeks? Two days? The same principle applies when exploring new careers. If you've dreamed of how glorious event planning could be, yet midway through your friend's wedding you're ready to drop your clipboard and run screaming from the chapel, that's telling you something.

Informational Interviews

This approach is one of my favorite ways to get information about a career. You can get an incredible amount of information in a short period of time. I requested over twenty informational interviews from people I didn't know when I was exploring careers, and was turned down by only one person.

Consider your audience when you make your request for an informational interview. Are you more likely to be able to reach them by snail mail, email, or telephone? I prefer the written form so that your target, especially if it's someone who doesn't know you, doesn't feel cornered by a telephone request. But if you already know the person and feel comfortable that they'd be happy to accept, go for it.

Between snail mail and email, the latter worked best for me, at least to start. I'd often send the email and mention that I'd follow up by telephone. In this day and age of spam, it can be difficult to ensure that your target receives the email, so it's always a good idea to follow up.

If someone can make an introduction for you, I highly recommend that approach. It is so much easier to reach busy people when you come vetted.

Make your requests as yes-able of a proposition as you can. Ask for thirty minutes of their time, over the telephone. Thirty minutes is not a substantial amount of time for them, but it is enough time for your purposes. And who doesn't find it easy just to answer the telephone when you call, rather than having to deal with traffic or whatever to meet you for coffee. The person can also do the call in pajamas if she so desires.

Be persistent. We can be so sensitive. We contact someone once, she doesn't respond, and we say sulkily, "Well, that's it. I guess she just doesn't want to help me." Not good enough. People are busy. Even if they want to help you, they have work, lives, children, errands, etc. You have to be persistent—polite but persistent. It took me a few months to get all twenty of those informational interviews scheduled.

And if you're feeling thin-skinned about it, that's okay. Do it anyway. Remember, the worse they can do is say no. As I said, I got one of those nos. Why someone can't spare thirty minutes to talk to someone, I don't know. But people are unpredictable. Maybe they fear you're going to ask them for a job, even though you explained that you wouldn't. Maybe they're feeling fragile about their career. Maybe they truly are overwhelmed. Or, maybe they're in the same position you are—in the wrong career. Or, heck, maybe they're just a jerk.

QUICK TIP

What questions to ask? Easy. You can use the ones from the interviews in this book. And don't forget to send the person a thank you note after the informational interview.

What now? Starting with the career possibility that excites you most, select the exploration ideas you like best and get going! It's best to pull out your calendar here and plot what you're going to do and when you're going to do it.

HAVE A LIST OF IDEAS, BUT STUCK IN DAYDREAMING MODE?

It's tempting to keep your dreams in your head where you can plot out how perfect your new career will be and how you will make the transition flawlessly. Visions are important, but if that's all you're doing, you may be buying into the *myth of motivation*. It's the myth that convinces us that we have to wait for a burst of inspiration to get started. It's time to explode that myth and get moving.

I have a similar fantasy about what it must be like to write a novel. You get up in the morning and walk to your tidy office with a cup of cocoa in hand. The characters of your novel are already dancing in your head, talking to you, urging you to get them onto the page. You turn on your computer, open to a blank page, and begin to write. You spend the morning writing a couple of chapters. You do it every day, and it's as easy as breathing.

When I share this vision with writers, they practically fall on the floor laughing.

I prefer my fantasy. Lovely, isn't it? And so unrealistic.

In order to uncover the career of your dreams, you're going to have to rely on teeth-gritting determination. Sure, there are times when you'll be in the flow, and the steps that you take to reach your goal will be effortless. Of course, make the most of those times.

But the majority of the time you may find yourself tired, cranky, and stuck. You're wondering if what you want for your work and your life are pipe dreams. If you're like my clients, you'll be thinking, "I just don't feel like it," or "I don't feel inspired."

That's when I ask a little question: are you exhausted and needing a break, or are you buying into the myth of motivation?

The *myth of motivation* is that in order to move forward with our goals, we must be inspired. If we're just not feeling it today, or we're betting this weekend we'll be motivated, we tell ourselves it's okay to wait.

If your answer to the question is, "I really am exhausted," then take a break. Most of my clients and readers are overachievers. They have crazy schedules and very little downtime. There are times when they have had the breath knocked out of them and need time to recover.

But if the truth is that you're buying into the myth of motivation, that's when it's time for what I call the *seat-of-the-chair approach*. I'm sure you've heard it before. Apply your pants to the seat of the chair and get something done. Anything.

I had to use this approach recently. I had a long list of things I needed to do, and I was feeling listless from the moment I woke up. Staying under that comforter was really tempting. I told myself, "I deserve this. I've been working really hard. I'm sure I'll be ready to go at it again tomorrow…"

And then I asked myself, "Are you tired, or are you just waiting on a visit from the Motivation Fairy?" Knowing the answer was the latter, I stomped out from under the comforter and flung myself into my office chair.

It's not pretty, but the seat-of-the-chair approach works wonders when applied diligently. Even if you're not in the mood to explore career possibilities, get to it. Oddly enough, that's often when the motivation appears.

HAVE A CAREER POSSIBILITY THAT FEELS SO FARFETCHED, YOU'RE AFRAID TO DIP YOUR TOE IN THE WATER?

Calling all hidden creative types!

Once upon a time, a college graduate with a BA in English and American Literature and tremendous potential pondered her career options. Growing up, she'd pursued a number of creative pursuits, from dance to playing violin to theater to a cappella to film. She was good at them all. She was also quite academically gifted and had grown up expecting to pursue a "real" career, but she just couldn't get herself excited about the traditional options offered at her career services office.

So she decided to resolve the question once and for all. She took a career aptitude test. Upon receiving the results, she ripped open the envelope and read the cryptic message:

Lawyer

Dancer

"Huh," the young girl said. She decided to become a lawyer—and most definitely did not live happily ever after.

Does this sound like the story of your life? I'm beginning to suspect that there are a lot of you creative types hiding out in the field of law. Why? Because that's who's calling me for career coaching. I've heard from lawyers who want to be jewelry designers, filmmakers, writers, and artists. Most of you whisper it, too, as if by saying it out loud, a gong will sound in your office, alerting everyone that you're an imposter.

And interestingly enough, most of you aren't even giving yourself the joy of playing in your creative field at all. You've put your so-called childish pursuits aside. I'm guilty of this, too. I didn't see the point of pursuing art for art's sake anymore, like I did when I was in school, so I put my ballet slippers in the closet when I became a lawyer.

What would it be like to immerse yourself in creative pleasures? Find out.

I'm talking about giving yourself permission to pursue some of the things you love, even if the outcome is just that you enjoy the doing of the thing itself and pursue it as a hobby.

If you feel stuck practicing law and are convinced you have no options, one of the ways you can get unstuck is to tap into your creativity. There's not necessarily an obvious connection here, such as if you start painting again, you may leave the law to become a painter full-time. That's a possibility, but opening yourself up creatively can also lead you in unexpected and unimaginable directions. What's needed is for you to open the door just a crack to your creativity and be curious about what you discover.

Now is the perfect time to flirt with the stuff you love. The following are a few ideas to get you going.

1. **Scrap the planning**. I'm going to recommend reckless abandon. No planning, no plotting, no what ifs. Select a creative pursuit strictly based on, "I think it'd be fun to __X__." Just fill in the blank. And be creative here—it doesn't necessarily have to be something artistic. "I think it'd be fun to learn how to surf" is a fair answer.

2. **Schedule some time**. It's the only analytical thing I'll allow you to do. Pull out your calendar and schedule eight to ten sessions over

the next couple of months. If all you have is fifteen minutes at 5:00 a.m. on Tuesdays, fine. Schedule it in. Don't feel like the only way to be a true artist is to schedule chunks of an hour or more.

3. **Pull out the paint and brushes and see what happens**. Just get going. Writers, open up to a blank page in your notebook or on your computer screen, pick your medium (short story, poem, article), and start writing. Jewelry designers, take a field trip to the bead store or other jewelry-making venue and gather your inspirational pieces.

4. **Get some accountability going**. Make this simple too. Tell a friend what you're up to. Better yet, buddy up with someone who also wants some creative play and keep an eye out for each other. I'm going to steal an idea from my own coach (Cynthia Morris, founder of life-coaching business Original Impulse), which she used to check in with me when I was exploring painting. After each of your scheduled appointments with creativity, email your buddy three adjectives to describe your experience. For example, "Painting today was exhilarating, fun, and frustrating."

LET ME CONTRADICT MYSELF

A freckled third grader with pigtails slouches at her desk looking out of the classroom window. She smiles as she envisions shapes in the fluffy white clouds. Crack! A book slams down on her desk. She starts and looks up into the thick spectacles of Mrs. Adams, her teacher. "Stop staring off into space, and pay attention! You'll never get anywhere by daydreaming!"

To the unimaginative, daydreaming seems like a waste of time. The old Nike® slogan admonishes us to "Just do it." Decide what you want, make a plan, and slog away until you get it done. But before you can do that, you've got to daydream. It is a crucial step on the path to fulfilling your career dreams.

"Now wait a minute," you say. "Didn't you just tell me to stop daydreaming and get moving?" I don't mean stop daydreaming altogether. Be selective about it. For example, daydreaming as a form of procrastination is not so good. If you're scared to move forward and you're relying on your daydreams because you get to be perfect in them, it's time to move on.

On the other hand, if you're daydreaming as a way of generating excitement and keeping your goal shining in your brain, that's a good thing. That kind of daydreaming is absolutely necessary.

Can you imagine Michelangelo or Benjamin Franklin creating and inventing without first having a vision? They must have spent time, and copious quantities of it, with their heads up in the clouds, envisioning what they wanted to achieve, before taking action.

You need an image for clarity. You need it to give you direction. And you are going to need it to do something grand, like leaving the law and pursuing the career of your dreams.

And once you have that image in your head, it sustains you throughout your adventure. You can call on it at any time and generate that same excitement, energy, and joy that you felt when you first defined your dream.

Some of us are so caught up in the day-to-day that we have forgotten how to daydream. Or we think daydreaming about how we can complete our errands in record time so we can sit down for a few minutes to breathe is it. It's not.

The stuff of real daydreams is grand visions—you sitting in the market of a French village painting, or laughing with Oprah as a guest on her show, or clipping the ribbon at the grand opening of your retreat center in New Mexico.

If you need some inspiration, some guidance on how to daydream, watch children when they're at rest. They become completely still, get a big, glazed look in their eyes, and chew on a finger or rest their chin on their hand. It may not last long, but that's a model for daydreaming.

WHAT TYPE ARE YOU?

Do you regard daydreamers warily and find comfort in your checklists? Or are you floating up there among the clouds, feet never coming down to the ground? You know yourself better than anyone. Most of us tend to fall into either one category or the other. Come clean. Whichever one you are, it's time to head on over to the dark side.

If You Pride Yourself on Taking Action

You have your list of career exploration ideas down, and you're steadily exploring them—that's great. Time to put the pad down and find a comfy chair, put your feet up on the ottoman, and practice daydreaming. Yes, to you practical types, this is a bit unnerving. So maybe you fall asleep the first few times, no big deal. There's no such thing as being perfect when it comes to daydreaming.

If You're the Daydreaming Champ

Get out of the comfy chair and go sit at your dining room table. Pull out a pad of paper, call a friend, get that list of career exploration ideas going, and tackle the first one on the list. Get out of your head and into the real world. Yes, I know in your head you get to make this perfect. But there's something exciting about the messy, unpredictable real world, too.

HARD TRUTH

This is work, isn't it? You were hoping this was going to be easy, weren't you? If you want easy, go find one of those lists that tells you what you can do with your legal degree, close your eyes, point at the list, and pursue whatever it is you put your finger on.

No one ever taught us how to do this. We went to grade school, elementary school, and high school, and all anyone said is, "What do you want to be when you grow up?" And you were supposed to know the answer! Then you go to college, choose a major, and everyone asks you the same question as you near graduation time. You pick law school because it's an easy option and the decision is pretty much made for you. How'd that work out?

No one showed us a process. Now I'm showing you a process, but it's not as easy as you thought it would be. Let me give you a word of advice I learned at the Citadel, the military college in South Carolina. I was part of a team that went in to help with the transition to coeducation. Being a cadet is challenging, especially the first year as you're transitioning to a military life. The upperclassmen can be very helpful in making that transition. Here are the comforting words of encouragement they give first-year cadets who are struggling—suck it up!

CASE STUDY
• • • • • • • • • • •

Cheryl Schneider, age 46
Pastry Chef and Owner, Penny Chocolates, Olney, Md.
2 years in pastry-making
BS in Telecommunication/Michigan State University
JD/American University
Years of practice: 17
Type of practice: international telecom, in-house, solo, and government in
*   D.C. Metro Area*

I don't want to ruin the suspense, but Cheryl's approach is a textbook illustration of ways to explore a career possibility. From treating her interest as a hobby, to taking a class or two or more, to being an apprentice—Cheryl dipped her toe in the water, then stepped in up to her knees, then took the plunge. It really is all about baby steps.

What I also love about Cheryl's approach is the importance of checking in with yourself to see if you are enjoying what you're exploring. Of course there are plans to make, obstacles to overcome, but it's too easy to let analysis or overanalysis paralyze you. For now, it's just about the joy of exploration. Let Cheryl's story inspire you to do just that.

Describe what you do.

In the pastry world there are people who do all kinds of different things. I focus on chocolate. I also make gelato and do a little bit of baking.

How did you get into chocolate-making?

It basically all started with a Christmas present that I got from my dad. This was in December 2000. I got a gift certificate from him to a local culinary school for a Christmas present. I had my eye on a particular class for a long time. I hemmed and hawed, and he said he was going to get me a gift certificate for the class. And I got it. I was busy; I was still practicing law, so I stuffed the gift certificate in a drawer and forgot about it.

And then I [was] cleaning out my office one day and I found the gift certificate. And I realized it was going to expire in about two days. I said, "Oh my gosh, well, I want to do something fun." So I picked up the phone, called, and signed up for the class I had wanted to take. It was a twenty-week intensive class in pastry. I took the class and that was really the beginning of the end of my law career. I just had such a good time in the class. I don't know. It just felt right.

The class was coming to an end and I just started to feel really sad. I approached the chef because he had a number of assistants who helped teach the class and asked, "Could you use another assistant?" He looked at me and thought a minute and said, "Okay, I'll take you." So I assisted him for about two years.

It was just one of those things that just slowly came over me. I took another class with one of the world-champion pastry chefs in chocolate and really liked that. [*Then Cheryl decided to attend an open house to see what the professional programs were like.*] I walked into the room, took one look at the pastry buffet, and burst into tears. I just knew that I just had to do this. That was where my heart was. That was it. It was over.

Later that year I ended up in culinary school as a full-time pastry arts student. It was a little strange. I was probably one of the oldest people in the class. There were some people right out of high school. I was the only lawyer. So that was a little bit odd, but I really enjoyed it. It was hard work and long hours. I had to go do an externship, which was a real eye-opener —going from a profession to a trade, being not only the low man on the totem pole, but the low man intern on the totem pole. But I just really loved it. I really enjoyed it.

When I got out of school in 2004 I started looking for a location [to open a chocolate store]. I knew I wanted to work for myself. After having spent seventeen years in corporations and dealing with all of the "great and wonderful people," as I call them, and all of the stress, I thought, "No, I want to work for myself. I want to be able to control my environment, to be able to have fun and do what I want." It took me about a year to find a space and get it set up. And I opened. I was in that space for about six months and thought, "Well, this isn't really the right space." Then I started looking and found a wonderful space.

It's kind of a funny story. Before I had gone to culinary school, I was making chocolates for friends and I was selling them as a fundraiser for the [National] AIDS Marathon.® I was in the lobby of an office building and a friend of mine who is a lawyer came down with his client. And the client had some chocolate and he looked at me and said, "If you ever want to open a retail store, call me," and he gave me his card.

Four years later I came across his card and said, "Well, let me just give him a call." Turns out that he was developing a shopping center in my town down the road from me and there was a historic tavern on the property they were going to renovate. He thought I was the perfect fit, so early next year I'm moving to a better location. So it's really one of those things that just kind of happened over the course of a couple of years.

It sounds like baby steps or little nudges or something.

Exactly. It was never one of those things where I sat down with a pile of books and analyzed everything and said, "Okay, I'm going to do this." I just wanted to enjoy myself. I wanted to do something I loved. So I just started doing that as a sideline, as a recreational activity, and the next thing I knew I was doing more and more. It just kind of took over.

What fears did you have about not practicing law?

I didn't really have any. As I said, I'd been working in international telecom for about seventeen years. I did a lot of traveling. I did a lot of neat things. And I just felt done. It wasn't that it wasn't an adjustment, but I just felt I had finished doing everything I wanted to do.

Define success.

For me, at this point it's really just being happy and having a profitable business. It's not anymore about getting that raise or that title or that office. I'm just really content. It doesn't take much for me to call it a success. I've really changed my view of the world. It's the little things.

How did you change your view of the world?

I think a lot of it is working in a different field with different people.

You're in an office with lawyers and everybody is a professional. You have support staff but they're all professional. It's very different.

And then you're in a kitchen with people who make $10 an hour. They work two or three jobs to make ends meet. And they're still really happy. You just learn that the money you get from being a lawyer [and] the whole ego thing just really doesn't matter.

You have to take the time to think about what you enjoy, what makes you happy. Once you key in on that, the status is irrelevant really.

How did you know this was the career for you?

It was baby steps, [I] just started working in the field. And I decided I really had the passion for it. Because it is very hard work, very long hours, and very physically demanding. Once I allowed myself to relax and explore things outside of law that I liked, I realized that this was the thing that just made me the happiest.

A lot of people like to cook, but you really have to have the passion. The chef [*her instructor*] used to say, "You have to have this little flame that burns inside, because if you don't have that, you're not going to make it because it is so tough."

If you look at the culinary world, pastry is the most detail-oriented. So it actually is a good fit if you're already a lawyer and very analytical, because in pastry everything matters. There is no such thing as an insignificant step. You can't just throw stuff in the pan or turn the oven on and not care what temperature it is. It's very analytical, very detail-oriented, very methodical. Even though it's creative, in a way it still really fit my personality.

What makes you different from lawyers who don't pursue their dreams?

I have a lot of chutzpah. You really have to have the guts or the courage to just take that leap of faith. And I didn't have any problems doing that. I figured, "Well, if it doesn't work out, I can always go back or I can do something else."

A lot of lawyers either become paralyzed at the thought of making the change or they overanalyze the situation. And they never feel comfortable about doing anything because they want one more piece of information or everything has to be lined up. To me, it felt right; I didn't overanalyze it. I thought, "You know, I'm going to do it. What the heck."

We [lawyers] like facts. We like data. We like information. We want to know all of the variations of what's going to happen, think through all the consequences. But sometimes you just can't. Sometimes you just have to do it.

What pressures did you experience to go the traditional route?

I had been in the [legal] field a long time. As my mother put it, "Well, you got your money's worth." I had done it for seventeen years. I didn't feel like I'd wasted it. I know some people feel that way. But I also feel that even if you practice for one or two years, the legal training that you get is so phenomenally useful in anything that you do, it's never a waste.

I got a great deal on my store lease because I could sit there and negotiate the agreement. I had a real estate attorney with me because it's not my area of expertise, but I know how to read a document. I understand how to put together a deal.

And also not being afraid to ask questions. Someone gives you a quote and you ask, "Wait a minute. What about this and this and this?" If you need regulatory clearance, not being afraid to pick up the phone and call the county and say, "What's going on? Help me do this." It's helpful. It's enormously helpful.

I'm a woman in business. In my case, a woman of color. People try to take advantage of you and act like you're stupid. You put that lawyer hat on and it just changes everything.

What doesn't appeal to you about practicing law?

A lot of it is so negative. Everything is adversarial. Everything is based on an issue or a problem. I'd just had enough of that negativity. And it just seemed to seep into everything, like the way people deal with each other. It just became really grating. No one could be nice, no one could be pleasant. Everything is competitive. I think, for me, I'd just really had enough.

In telecom too, things changed tremendously. So everything became about price. It used to be kind of clubby, very congenial, fun. With the growth in the industry and the pressure on prices a lot of companies weren't making the margins they used to. I just had enough of that.

Now I can focus my energy on positive things. I get to create stuff. People are so happy when they walk in the door of my store. They say, "Thank you." No one ever thanks their lawyer.

What's the purpose of work in your life?

I have to make a living. But other than that, because I love what I do it doesn't feel like work. "Oh, I get to make such-and-such today." Or I'm working on a new recipe that's a challenge. It's just not work for me.

And what's nice about having the store too is that my kids can come in the store and work with me. My family can come in the store and work with me. It's something we can all do together. And for my children, it's great because they understand what I do. [Before it was] "Oh, Mom's a lawyer. I don't know what she does. She goes to her office."

Anything else you want to share?

I get so many people that say, "Wow, congratulations, how'd you do it?" or "Oh, you got out." I don't think that people should be afraid to try. The nice thing about law is you can pretty much always go back. Maybe not to that exact same job, but you're employable. You're not going to starve. So just take the chance.

· · · · · · · · · · · · ·

WHAT YOU SHOULD HAVE LEARNED IN THIS CHAPTER

- ☐ Be bold and go where most unhappy lawyers have not gone before to find fulfilling work outside the law.

- ☐ If you're waiting on the motivation fairy, you'll be waiting awhile. Get started and the motivation might just show up.

- ☐ Use your daydreams to give you power and courage and keep your vision alive.

- ☐ If you love it, if you enjoy it—those are vital signs that you just shouldn't ignore.

chapter four

What Do You Think?

LETTER FROM A DESPERATE LAWYER

Dear Monica,

I really love flowers. I read a novel once about a lawyer who left the practice of law and opened a flower shop. I'd love to do that. My neighborhood florist lets me hang around in her shop on weekends and I have a ball. But everybody makes fun of me for wanting to enjoy myself at work. They say that's why work is called "work" and not "play." What do you think?

Lauren

Decisions, decisions. Do your dreams make sense or are they crazy? Is what you're thinking about a good idea or a disaster? All you want is for someone to tell you what career you should pursue next. Guess what? The only person who can tell you that is *you*. Rather than waiting for the divine sign, there are intuitive and practical approaches you can use to help you move forward.

WHAT DOES YOUR GUT SAY ABOUT THE CAREER POSSIBILITIES?

With each career option you explore, check in with yourself. This is not the time to analyze. You are simply checking in with your gut, your intuition, and your heart to see what they have to say.

Gut-Checking Process

1. Right after you explore a career possibility, jot down your reactions. You could do a fifteen-minute free write or call your buddy, and let it all gush out like when you were a kid.

2. Go through this gut-checking process often as you are exploring each career possibility on your list.

Checking in with your intuition is key to the career exploration process. If you had checked in with your intuition while you were in law school, you probably would have run screaming from Civil Procedure and never come back. I'll never forget when I got into law school and got the course catalogue. I flipped through it and thought, "Wow, all of these classes look really boring."

The same holds true now. If you follow a florist around for a day and wake up that afternoon with your head in the cooler, that's what's called a warning sign. If you finish your introductory dirt bike racing class and immediately sign up for the rest of the series, that's saying something else.

Warning! Check In With Your Gut, *Not* Your Head

Remember when I said this is not the time to analyze? Some of you promptly ignored that advice and began immediately telling yourself why the career possibility that fascinates you is just not going to happen. Let me introduce you to that smooth talker. Reader, this is your *Gremlin*.[8]

[The Gremlin] is the narrator in your head. He tells you who you are, and he defines and interprets your every experience. He wants you to feel bad, and he pursues this loathsome task by means of sophisticated maneuvers; just when you feel you've out-argued or overcome him, he changes his disguise and his strategy. He's the sticky sort—grapple with him and you become more enmeshed. What he hates is simply being noticed. That's the first step to his taming.[9]

Those are the intriguing words from *Taming Your Gremlin: A Guide to Enjoying Yourself* by Richard Carson, creator of the powerful yet whimsical metaphor for your internal voice.

There are several other names for the Gremlin—the internal censor, the voice inside your head, the committee, the internal saboteur.

Your Gremlin wants to stop you in your tracks the minute you dare to contemplate this journey. Why? Because it abhors change. It wants to keep you safe, and safety is best preserved by keeping you exactly where you are. Never mind that you're miserable. "If you leave, you'll be even more miserable because you'll have made a terrible mistake," your Gremlin warns.

Don't argue with your Gremlin. You can't win. Right now, your focus should be on your gut and not the voice in your head trying to talk you out of this process. Your gut usually has lots of wildly improbable, exciting things to say. It likes to blurt stuff out. It's got the exuberance and bluntness of a 6-year-old. It says things like, "I love it!" "I hate it!" "I'm never doing *that* again!"

My Own Gut-Checking Experiments

I spent lots of time daydreaming about a career in interior design. I'd already conducted an informational interview with an interior designer who loved his job. I was sure it'd be a perfect fit for me. I also knew I needed a reality check—a chance to see what the day-to-day life of an interior designer was like. I was delighted when that same interior designer offered to let me tag along with him for a day.

We went to a client's home to review ongoing renovations to her sleek, minimalist kitchen. We met with a client at his office to draft designs for a gorgeous new office space. We also visited showroom after showroom piled high with luxurious Oriental rugs to find the perfect design for another client. My gut reaction? Boring! I was drained by the end of the day. Not the career for me.

Contrast that experience with when I explored coaching. I signed up for a coach training course. The class was a full three days. At the end of the course, as I was driving home, I noticed I was practically bouncing around in the car from all the energy I had. My past work experiences usually left me drained and exhausted. I was so excited. All I kept thinking was—I want that! This was a very different experience from my exploration of interior design.

STOP WAITING FOR THE LIGHTBULB MOMENT

We all know those folks who have known since they were 6 years old what they wanted to do. Or perhaps you've heard of a lawyer who had a life-changing experience and changed her career in the blink of an eye and lived happily ever after. It could happen to you. Or not. Do not sit around waiting for it.

We're not all going to experience an instantaneous transformation. In fact, that's a dangerous dream to pursue. Transformation, at least meaningful and sustained transformation, is a process, not a one-time event.

My transformation from lawyer to coach wasn't a whirlwind romance. It took place over a span of five years. For starters, I was exploring a number of possibilities at the same time, not just coaching. I was gathering as many experiences as possible in careers that interested me. I was meeting new people in those professions and envisioning what my life would be like if I was a part of their community. I was also freaking out about making a career change, wondering if giving up the legal profession would be the biggest mistake of my life, and stalling.

Now don't panic. I'm not telling you that you have to wait five years before you can move on. What I'm telling you is that changing careers is a messy, creative process that often involves one step forward and two steps back. Sometimes you'll be bold and take big leaps; other times, you'll move forward tentatively.

It's not about thinking really hard and coming up with exactly what you want to do, either. Nor is it about taking an assessment that spits out the career for you. Those are stifling notions about how to make a career change. Instead, it's about discovering what career possibilities excite you, trying them on, and getting to know people in those professions. It's about figuring out what the roadblocks are and making choices about which of those you want to overcome and which you don't.

In her book *Working Identity: Unconventional Strategies for Reinventing Your Career*, Herminia Ibarra argues for this unconventional approach: "While common wisdom holds that we must first know what we want to do before we can act…this advice is backward. Knowing…is the result of *doing* and *experimenting*. Career transition is not a straight path toward some predetermined identity, but a crooked journey along which we try on a host of 'possible selves' we might become."[10]

What are these *possible selves* Ibarra speaks of? The *possible selves* are who we could become next in our career path. For example, when I decided to change careers, I made a list of career possibilities.

- Maybe there's some way I could use my legal degree that would be appealing. Legal recruiting, teaching the law, career services at a law school, or going back into conflict resolution work since that's a legal discipline.

- I loved dance all through grade school and college. I'm probably too old to be a dancer now, but maybe I could get involved with a dance company somehow.

- I could get back into film development.

- I love books. I could become a literary agent. (That's not an unusual transition for a lawyer.)

- Maybe consulting. Lots of lawyers transition to that.

- I could try another practice area.

- I love food, especially dessert. Maybe there's something I could do that would allow me to be surrounded by chocolate.

- My mom has always seen me as a high-powered attorney at a fancy firm. Wearing sharp suits and heels and doing big deals. As much as that image repulses me, success on that level still intrigues me.

- I'd like my own business. Maybe a combination of coaching, training, speaking. I could work with lawyers like me.

- Maybe I could be a writer. Nonfiction, mystery. Maybe it's time to try my hand at it.

Ibarra would comment that the list is telling because it reflects my possible selves—finding a compromise within the field of law that I could live with (reasonable, practical self), rekindling my childhood dreams of dance or film (old fantasy self), fantasies of becoming a writer (today's fantasy), and high-powered attorney (an example of selves seen by others who know me and my talents well).

Ibarra would also say that my list:

> looks like countless others. A possible-selves list always has a favorite (and it is always near the bottom of the list, as if we were fearful of even exposing it). The list often starts with what gets framed as the 'reasonable option,' one that exploits the past but in a new context or job. The tone used to describe this path betrays its lack of appeal. The list typically has something on it we really do not want to do. Sometimes it has role models, people whom we would like to be like. More often than not, it also has things we really have no intention of actually exploring but that add color to the list or are thrown in to round things out. What are we to do with such a list? We start to act, in order to find out what to cross off and what to explore.[11]

Maybe you try one possibility out by taking on a few projects, and decide, "This isn't for me." Maybe another intrigues you, but it doesn't seem like the right move for now. Or perhaps you make a connection with someone in a field that interests you, and begin to see similarities between yourself and her.

It's about seeing what you like and what you don't like. It's a process of discovery, not just about the career, but also about who you are and what you want from your work and your life.

It's counterintuitive, I know. We've been fed a steady diet of, "Think about it really hard and you can figure out what you want to do." I'm asking you to put that notion aside and act. Just take action, explore, experience, react. What you want to do is going to emerge from that creative process.

YOU'RE DOING MORE THAN CHANGING JOBS—YOU'RE CHANGING YOUR WORKING IDENTITY

Changing careers is about more than moving from Point A to Point B. If it were just a mechanical exercise, it would be easy. What also has to happen is that your mind has to be transformed. You have to make the shift from seeing yourself as a lawyer to seeing yourself as many other possibilities. You have to build a bridge from who you are now to who you want to be. That often takes time and, more importantly, a mental shift.

Ibarra describes it this way:

> We like to think that the key to a successful career change is knowing what we want to do next and then using that knowledge to guide our actions. But change usually happens the other way around: Doing comes first, knowing second. Why? Because changing careers means redefining our working identity—how we see ourselves in our professional roles, what we convey about ourselves to others, and ultimately, how we live our working lives.

> Most of the time, our working identity changes so gradually and naturally that we don't even notice how much we have changed. But sometimes we hit a period when the desire for change imposes itself with great urgency. What do we do? We try to think out our dilemma. We try to swap our old, outdated roles for new, more alluring selves in one fell swoop. And we get stuck. [A more successful way of making the change is to] rethink ourselves...by gradually exposing ourselves to new worlds, relationships, and models.[12]

Just look at how you became a lawyer, for example. It was a gradual process—thinking about going to law school, taking the LSAT, applying to schools, spending three years learning to think like a lawyer, taking the bar exam, starting practice. That's very different, I would imagine, from how you'd like to approach your career change now. You want out and you want out quickly. So you're looking for a magical cure. You suspect that if you think about your situation very hard, you will come up with a solution. You will be able to make your career change overnight. Lawyers I've spoken to who have tried to reinvent themselves that quickly—say, those who attempt to go from practicing lawyer to painter overnight—either scare themselves so much that they become paralyzed or they make a leap that they either regret or wish they'd spent some time gradually shifting into. So I'll say it again—*this change is going to take some time and a mental shift.*

QUICK TIP

Feeling totally freaked out at this point? If so, that means that in spite of everything I've just said, you may be obsessing, "I *have* to figure this out before I make a move." You're putting too much pressure on yourself. A lot of my clients get caught up in asking themselves what they should do for the rest of their lives. That's a heavy question. Who says you have to figure out what you're doing for the rest of your life?

If that's what you're thinking, take the pressure off. Ask simply, what do I want to explore next? That gives you the freedom to make mistakes. It gives you the freedom to try something out, see if it works, and move on if it doesn't.

WHAT IF IT TURNS OUT YOU REALLY WANT TO FOLLOW MORE THAN ONE CAREER PATH?

Some of you fall into a special category. You have a dirty little career secret. The secret is that you don't want to spend the rest of your life pursuing one career. In fact, you'd be bored and restless if someone tried to force you to do that. When you are dreaming without any inhibitions, you dream about what it would be like to pursue one career, then give that one up and pursue another, then another.

Welcome to the wonderful world of Scanners.[13] Barbara Sher coined the term *Scanner* in her book, *Refuse to Choose*:

> [A Scanner is] a very special kind of thinker. Unlike those people who seem to find and be satisfied with one area of interest, you're genetically wired to be interested in many things, and *that's exactly what you've been trying to do.* Because your behavior is unfamiliar—even unsettling—to the people around you, you've been taught that you're doing something wrong and you must try to change....What you've assumed is a disability to be overcome by sheer will is actually an exceptional gift. You are the owner of a remarkable, multitalented brain trying to do its work in a world that doesn't understand who you are and doesn't know why you behave as you do.[14]

I almost dropped Sher's book in shock when I read this passage because it was as if it was written just for me. All you'd have to do is look at my résumé to confirm that I am a Scanner. I started my career in film, then shifted to grocery store management, to law, to conflict resolution, back to law, then to coaching. And I had a sneaking, uncomfortable suspicion that even after I discovered coaching, this career wouldn't be the end of the ride for me—that I would never actually settle down in one career but would pursue as many as was humanly possible. I'd even come to an uneasy truce with myself that this was the way I was built, in spite of the fact that it looked like the rest of society was going in the opposite direction.

Now even if your résumé doesn't look like mine, it doesn't mean that you're not a Scanner. Whether you act on the impulse to reinvent yourself or resolutely trudge forward in the same career, even though the idea of staying in that one career for the rest of your life makes you miserable, you're on my team. Or it could be that you're fascinated by something new every week, can't commit to anything because you're afraid you'll miss something better, or you start so many things but finish almost none of them. All symptoms of a Scanner, according to Sher.

Based upon my conversations with clients and other lawyers, I suspect that there may be a number of you who are Scanners. "What does this mean?!" you demand. Are you doomed to go through life never choosing a career, never enjoying the stability that the rest of society has? Depends upon your definition of stability, I'd say. You can fight your nature or you can accept it.

HARD TRUTH

If you're stuck here—can't think of possibilities, paralyzed as to where to go—there's something else going on. You may be feeling guilty. You've worked so hard to get to this point—the LSATs, law school, the bar, interviews, and, possibly, partnership—and now you're going to give it all up. And for some of us, becoming a lawyer represents an opportunity that our family, our race, our gender hasn't had in the past. That you would give all of this up for happiness, peace, fulfillment (?!) is unfathomable to some people. And secretly, it's almost unfathomable to you.

You tell yourself you should be grateful for your job. You have a good salary that allows you to meet your expenses and have a few luxuries. This is absolutely something to be grateful for. What does not make sense is taking that gratitude and using it as a weapon against yourself—scolding yourself for being ungrateful, telling yourself you have no right to be unhappy and to want to leave the law.

Here's what else we have to be thankful for—that we have the opportunity to make choices, that we can choose work that's fulfilling. That if we want to leave the law to pursue work that's meaningful to us, we can do just that.

So of course be grateful for your job. And know that if you choose to do something else with your JD, something that fulfills you, you can be even more grateful.

CASE STUDY

• • • • • • • • • • • •

Amy Gutman, age 47

Serial Careerist; Special Assistant to the Dean for Communications, Director of Alumni Communications and Special Projects, Harvard Law School, Cambridge, Mass.

1½ years in strategic communications and project planning

BA in History and Literature/Harvard College

JD/Harvard Law School

Years of practice: 4

Type of practice: litigation, large firm, and entertainment boutique in New York, N.Y.

Wondering what that title *serial careerist* is all about? It's what Amy calls herself because of her varied résumé. She has been a copy editor, reporter, novelist, lawyer, and has worked for a state department of education. Amy also describes herself as an *experience junkie*. She has taken on positions—including her job practicing law at a big, prestigious law firm—purely for the experience of it. She says, "I wasn't likely to think, 'Is this job a good fit?' I just thought, 'Wow, I want to see that.'" She says that approach has driven her career decisions a lot of times.

In fact, Amy is a Scanner. Whatever you call it, if you're this type of person, it's incredibly reassuring to know that there are other lawyers like you out there who have careers that they enjoy. If you're wondering whether your inability to stick with a career means that you're a hopeless case, Amy's story shows that you don't have to choose just one career for the rest of your life and that there's nothing wrong with you.

Describe what you do.

[As the Special Assistant to the Dean for Communications] I do a lot of high level communications work involving articulating the Dean's vision for the law school.

On the other side [in the Director of Alumni Communications and Special Projects position], I launched the law school's alumni e-newsletter.

One of the things I was interested in was that there were a lot of opportunities to create more synergies and more of a sense of community with Harvard Law School alums. I thought one way to do that would be to have a publication essentially devoted to ways alums could connect with the law school.

I'm very much project-oriented. The big project I'm working on now is *Celebration 55: The Women's Leadership Summit,* which will be the law school's convocation of women alums. So I'm developing programming and reaching out in terms of putting that together.

What I'm really interested in is using communications strategically and building community. Those are the two things that drive me. And I try to find ways that they connect with the law school's priorities and my colleagues' priorities.

Describe serial careerist.

If you look at my résumé, I've just done one thing after another. I have not historically stayed with things more than a couple of years. Except my writing. I did do that for a five-year block, but that was working for myself essentially. But in work places I've tended to do things in shorter spurts. Which I think is becoming increasingly common as a career path.

When I was still writing [novels] I used to joke that I was "a serial careerist who wrote about serial killers." But of course I'm not doing that anymore because I'm a serial careerist.

Have you heard of Barbara Reinhold? She wrote a wonderful book, *Free to Succeed: Designing the Life You Want in Today's Free Agent Economy.* When I was going through my career transition, I met with her several times. She looked at my résumé and said, "Well, you have a short career metabolism." I said, "What?!" She said, "You do one thing for five years and then you have to do something else. That's how you are."

And I'd been feeling like, "What's wrong with me? Why can't I just find something that I like and stick with it?" I thought writing would be it and that I'd want to do it forever and even that I didn't want to stick with.

[Reinhold] said, "There's good news and bad news. The good news is you'll have a very interesting life and the bad news is it can be sort of rocky at times."

Being in a job now where I can do more different things within the job is helping me. That's because I've got a lot of freedom on the job. I've been able to initiate more things and I've got a good relationship with my boss and the Dean. The job was created for me and is still very much a work in progress.

How did you get into strategic communications and project planning? Since you've already described yourself as having a short career metabolism and I'm suspecting I may have readers like that, let's back this up to when you graduated from college.

When I got out [of college] I didn't know what I wanted to do. I had been on the *Crimson* [Harvard College's newspaper], although not particularly active. But writing had always been something that was a core thing for me. So I got an internship at a magazine in Washington, D.C., and ended up being hired to be their copy editor.

From there [I] took a reporting job. I had a friend who was a reporter in the Deep South and I was fascinated by that. So I went to work for a paper in Tennessee. Then I decided I needed to go even farther south. I went to Mississippi. I was hired to work for a paper; then, I was doing freelance work.

After that, I was hired by the state higher education commissioner. [*Complaining about the fact that she had lots of friends who'd like to teach in Mississippi but couldn't because they didn't have teaching certifications, Amy learned that the state legislature had passed an alternative certification model that was little known at the time. She designed the Mississippi Teacher Corps, wrote the grant, and recruited teachers. The program ended up getting national publicity and continues today.*]

And then I came up to Harvard Law School. Going to Harvard Law seemed like a way to get back on track in a way. [What I'd done up to this point] seemed like a somewhat eccentric career path and I wasn't sure how to reconnect.

So I came to law school with the thought that I'd go into some sort of policy, education-related thing. I hadn't come up here with a fervent commitment to do that though. So then when all the big firm stuff started happening, I just thought, I'd never made any money at all. Also when I went to New York to interview (because that's what people were doing) I just sort of fell in love with the city. I just thought, "I want to do this." It was really about moving to New York, as much as it was practicing law, which is sort of a funny thing to say if you're going to a really high-level, challenging law firm.

So I went [to a big law firm in New York]. I certainly didn't think that I would stay there and become a partner. And I didn't. So I left after two years there—it was a challenging environment and I wasn't someone who was cut out for large firm life. It's an environment that does work for some people, but it wasn't one that was going to be the right place for me long-term.

That's when I started to think seriously about trying to write. I'd started reading a lot of thrillers as I was practicing law. I'd always been more of a nineteenth-century literature reader, but it was almost like a yin-yang kind of thing. I was doing something incredibly arduous and demanding during the work day. I wanted to do something totally frivolous at night.

Also the partner I'd gone to work for [at the firm] died. So that was very sad. And I felt like he'd been my real connection.

I decided it was time to move on and I got a part-time job working at this entertainment boutique with the idea that I would try to write a novel. I did that for about a year and it was fun, but I wasn't actually doing that much writing. And my bank account was dwindling. So I decided that I needed to go back to work full-time.

So I went back full-time and I had a really interesting case during that time. I was the lead associate on a case challenging the authorship of a musical. It got a lot of press coverage and was really interesting. We won at trial.

I remember right after that I started thinking. [During a firm celebration for the win] one of my best friends there bounced into my office and said sourly [but humorously], "So how does it feel to know that this is as good as it gets?" I thought, "That's true. I'm never going to have a case that's as interesting as this again." I was really grateful for the experience and felt really good about the result, but I also had this tugging feeling. I thought, "Is this really what I want to spend my life doing?"

[*Amy was also influenced by the writer of the musical. When he died, there'd been a challenge to the authorship, hence the lawsuit. Amy read a lot of his journals as her firm handled the case. He spoke of being devoted to living life at the fullest. She wrote the brief on appeals in that case and shortly after that left the firm.*]

I'd started looking at other law firms, other jobs, and realized there just wasn't anything. I didn't have a lot of faith that I would be able to write and publish a book, but by this point I did have some savings. I said I would give myself a year and if it didn't work out, I'd do something else. (I'm reading that Ibarra book [*Working Identity*] now and it's very much about living your way into the next thing and I was sort of doing that.)

But then as it happened, amazingly enough, I did end up selling the book. I think I was down to my last $5,000, which is terrifying to think about. I got this six-figure book deal—it was actually a two-book deal—and then wrote for the next four or five years. It shouldn't have taken me that long to write two books, but it did. [*Amy wrote two legal thrillers,* Unequivocal Death *and* The Anniversary.] That was just a wild ride, really exciting.

But then when I came to my third book I was having a lot of trouble coming up with something. I thought, "What am I going to do? Am I going to do this for the rest of my life?" At that point I just felt that I'd done what I'd set out to do, which was publish a book.

I wanted a life that was less exhausting and stressful on a day-to-day basis. And I wanted a job. I didn't want a law practice job where I was going to be working eighty hours a week. But I wanted something that would give me stability and something that would allow me to write if I wanted to write, but where I wouldn't feel like I couldn't pay my rent if I wasn't writing.

Then I started thinking about all the times I'd changed careers and I came up with the idea that I should be in an academic environment because I felt there'd be more options and more potential diversity [of work] within the institution. So I started looking for jobs of various types at colleges and universities. [*Amy joined Harvard Law as the Assistant Director for Academic Affairs, but that turned out not to be a good fit.*] I started doing some writing for the Dean and that led to this other job. [*Over a series of months Amy pitched several job possibilities to her then-boss, who was very supportive, and finally created a position for herself.*] As I said, it's still a work in progress. But neither of my titles existed before. There was a need but there wasn't really a job.

What fears did you have about not practicing law?

I'm not sure I did [have fears] to the extent that other people did because I had a whole career before [law school]. It's almost more surprising that I ever worked at a law firm. I did not at all plan to be a partner. I don't think that was even on my radar screen. So the fact that I went to a law firm and did the traditional legal practice thing is more surprising than that I left.

Define success.

Happiness. But in a very nonsuperficial way. I'm sort of an intermittent—consistently intermittent, I'd say—Buddhist practitioner. One of the core teachings is that all beings wish to be happy. That's the starting point. I think we become happy by caring about the happiness of others, as well as our own. Happiness isn't about buying stuff or whatever. I mean happiness [as] equated with serenity, peace of mind, such that you're doing the right thing.

How did you know this was the career for you? Funny question to ask a serial careerist, I think.

I think I know it's the career for me now because I feel basically happy (in the way that I'm using the term "happiness") about what I'm doing and engaged.

I can't imagine I will be here forever, for the rest of my career. I'm certainly not averse to doing it but I think that there tend to be shifts in my career certainly and I think increasingly in most people's careers.

Say more about being engaged.

By engaged I mean that I'm working for something that's in synch with my values, which are building community and creating these connections. I think our Dean is doing such an amazing job with the direction of the law school, the messages that she puts out in the world. Just even what the law school is doing itself, in terms of the environment, human rights, all of these different areas that are going to so much determine the future of the planet. So I feel good to be a part of that. That's the values piece.

But then if I were being a part of that by doing filing, that wouldn't cut it. So the other piece of it is being a part of it in ways that engage my signature strengths, which are creativity, ingenuity, and originality; curiosity and interest in the world; judgment, critical thinking, and open-mindedness; humor, playfulness, and love of learning. I feel like, yeah, my job really does use these things.

But also aligned with my values. If I were doing all of these things, I don't know, advertising for cars, that for me wouldn't be sufficiently aligned with my values.

What makes you different from lawyers who don't pursue their dreams?

That's a hard one because I don't know if I'm in a position to say who is or who isn't [pursuing their dreams].

If people feel like they have dreams and are stymied and wonder, "Why is that?" there's a line from a former guru of a Kripalu ashram. He said, "Company is stronger than willpower." What I think it means is, who you hang out with is going to have a much stronger impact on your actions than any effort you could possibly exert to make yourself do something. If you're hanging out with people who are following their dreams, it's going to come much easier for you. If you're hanging out with people who don't share your values or vision, you could just berate yourself 'til the cows come home and it's still going to be really hard for you to feel like this is doable and reasonable. So I think surrounding yourself with people who share your values, support you, and think you can do it is one of the critical pieces.

What pressures did you experience to go the traditional route?

I actually think not so much because even in my era there were people visible going into public interest work. I really did want the experience and the stability [of practicing at a firm]. And the money was—I was 33 at that point, and I'd never really made any money. I just didn't want to give up that opportunity to make a reasonable amount of money for a while. So I think that was internal; that wasn't about peer pressure.

What doesn't appeal to you about practicing law?

I have a friend who was president of Harvard Law Review and he's now a journalist. He says, "Law. You know, it's interesting, but it's just not that interesting." I do find it interesting. [Laughter.] I find it interesting to write about. I find the issues compelling. But I needed something broader. And I also wanted more control over my time than a traditional legal practice allowed.

What's the purpose of work in your life?

Well, paying my bills. And feeling that I'm making a contribution. I'm someone who, if I see a problem, likes to find a creative way to address it. So I get to do that and I find a lot of satisfaction in that.

Anything else you want to share?

I did not come out with any significant law school debt and I think that's important to put out on the table. I was very fortunate in that way.

I hear that the average debt now is something around $100,000. That's an issue. It's not to say you still can't do it. I think the worse thing, though, is when people start beating themselves up for not following their dreams. It's so not helpful. Give yourself a break. Recognize that just because you're not doing it now doesn't mean you won't ever do it.

• • • • • • • • • • • • •

WHAT YOU SHOULD HAVE LEARNED IN THIS CHAPTER

☐ Trust the gut, not the Gremlin.

☐ What's that expression—you couldn't think your way out of a paper bag? You can't think your way out of your legal career either. Act!

☐ Michelangelo, Benjamin Franklin, and Amy Gutman, who you just read about in the Case Study, are Scanners. That's some pretty cool company.

chapter five

Time to Let Your Left Brain Out of Its Cage: Planning How to Make Your Great Escape

---

LETTER FROM A DESPERATE LAWYER

Dear Monica,

I'd like to leave. But I have a lot of doubts. I mean, a lot. How do you get past stuff like that?

Matt

If your left brain is anything like mine, it's roaring to be released. It's saying things like, "What's all this check in with your gut, intuition crap? Let me at those dreams of yours!"

It's time to release the beast. I call the left brain a beast because it tends to be a dream crusher. But here's the thing. You've been given a left brain and a right brain for a reason. If the two work in tandem, they can be quite a team. You need the left brain to help you determine what is possible and what is not possible. You just need a way to keep it under control.

One of the best ways I've discovered to integrate the left brain into the process is the 1-2-3 career counseling process[15] described by Howard Figler and Richard Bolles in their book, *The Career Counselor's Handbook.*

SIMPLE, BUT NOT EASY

Remember the Indiana Jones movie *Raiders of the Lost Ark*? That's what leaving the law feels like for a lot of us—a complicated, mysterious, and dangerous treasure hunt. We know the ark (i.e., our dream job) is out there, but it seems only fair that we should at least have some sort of treasure map that would give us a sense of direction through the scary terrain of career change.

I found the treasure map and now I'm going to bequeath it to you. Be fore-warned—it's so simple and obvious that you might not see its value. It *is* obvious, but it's also incredibly profound.

Figler and Bolles say that the themes of career counseling are captured in three questions.

1. What do I want to do?

2. What's stopping me?

3. What am I doing about it?

Everything you need to know to keep you on track is right here. As you go through the career transition process, you will go back and forth among these three questions.

I told you it was simple. But again, don't dismiss it out of hand. Here's what Figler and Bolles have to say about it:

> Is [changing careers] 'as easy as 1-2-3'? Not hardly. On the contrary, these questions confront [career changers] with the complexity of their motivation, their struggle to keep themselves on track, the effort required to stay focused, the various motivations that confuse them, and the subtleties of understanding who they really are.[16]

In a nutshell, the three questions are simple, but they're not easy.

We've covered the first question, "What do I want to do?" in great detail already. Remember, it's not about having crystal clarity around this question. It's just, what are the possibilities that excite you? Let's dig into the other two questions.

WHAT'S STOPPING YOU?

Now here is where the left brain gets to go to town. It's also the question all my clients can answer without any hesitation. These are all the obstacles in the way of you being able to do "X." Figler and Bolles call these the "Yes, Buts."[17] You have to get them out so you can see how realistic they are. A lot of times they're overblown, but sometimes there's some grain of reality there. You have to know what that grain is so you can decide if it's worth overcoming.

Here are some of the typical Yes, Buts.

- **Lack of money.** "I don't have the money to go back to school." "I can't take a job that pays less than six figures. I've gotten used to this lifestyle." "I have loans. It'll take me years to save up enough to start my own business and have enough to live on."

- **Lack of experience.** "I'd have to go back to school and get another degree and I'm not about to do that."

- **Lack of time.** "I have a husband, three kids, a dog, a home we're renovating, a full-time job, I teach Sunday School, I volunteer at Habitat for Humanity…"

- **Family obligations.** "My parents will think I'm crazy." "I have to care for my aging grandmother, so this just isn't a possibility right now." "I'm the breadwinner for my family. I'm single but everyone in my immediate family—my mom, brothers and sisters, cousins—relies on me in emergency situations."

- **Fear.** "I'm afraid I'll fail. What if I fall on my face?" "I'm afraid of what others will say—my family, my friends, my firm." "What if I make the wrong career choice?" "I'm afraid of letting go of my status as a lawyer."

What other concerns do you have? Get them all out. This is the left brain's chance to bring up every possible reason why what you want isn't possible.

Whenever I do this exercise with clients, they're deflated. The obstacles seem insurmountable. That's not the end of the exercise, though, so hang on.

WHAT ARE YOU DOING ABOUT IT?

My clients definitely do not like this question. I'm not the only one who harbors the secret dream that when we figure out what we want to do, all obstacles will be blown out of our path. Some of them will be, but for others we have to figure out a way around, over, or through them.

This is where the true warriors become evident. Either you find a way to blast through the obstacles, or you say, "Nah, too much for me" and circle back to the first question, "What do I want to do?" Both approaches are honorable; the only loss is if you give up.

In answer to the question, "What am I doing about it?" Figler and Bolles recommend *reality testing*.[18] There are two types of *reality tests*.

1. **Type A:** How accurate is my perception of the problem? How can I get better data?

2. **Type B:** If Type A reality testing shows the obstacle is real, what can I do to improve my situation and begin overcoming the obstacle?

I've devoted a whole chapter (Chapter Seven) to the lack of money excuse. If that's your big obstacle, skip ahead and read that section. For now, let's do some reality testing on a family obligation excuse.

"I'm the Breadwinner for My Family. I'm Single But Everyone in My Immediate Family—My Mom, Brothers and Sisters, Cousins—Relies on Me in Emergency Situations."

Here is a conversation between me and a client, Gillien, reality testing this Yes, But.

MP: Okay, how accurate is your perception of the problem? [*Reality Test Type A*]

GILLIEN: It's pretty accurate. It's not that anyone in my family is lazy—well, one of my sisters is a bit. Anyway, it's more that I'm the one in the family who's "made something of her life." I have a big salary and since I'm single, it's not like I have any other obligations. Or at least that's how my family feels.

MP: How do you feel?

GILLIEN: I guess in some sense I like having people rely on me. I like being able to help. But there are also times I feel resentful. I had to cancel a vacation once because my brother got caught up in some mess and, being the lawyer, I had to get involved. That really pissed me off. I work hard; I deserved to have some time off. On the other hand, my family needed me.

MP: Sounds like a tug of war of the heart.

GILLIEN: Yeah, that's it. I love my family and I feel a sense of obligation to them. But I don't like it that this obligation overruns my own needs.

MP: What are your needs?

GILLIEN: To have a little space, some peace and quiet. To not be on twenty-four-hour call. To not have to worry all the time. I mean, can't these people take some responsibility for themselves?

MP: Every family has its own dynamics. Each member has his or her own role, established in childhood. It's hard changing those roles.

GILLIEN: Yeah, my role is mediator. I've always been the mediator. Something goes wrong, I try to smooth things over. I'm tired of being the mediator!

MP: What do you want to be? What role do you want to have? [*Reality Test Type B*]

GILLIEN: I want to have a normal family. I want people to stop pressuring me to fix things.

MP: It'd be nice if we could make other people change. Not really possible though, is it? We, on the other hand, can change. Who do you want to be in this family?

GILLIEN: Oh, I see what you're saying. Who do I want to be? Hmmm… that's hard. I want to be kind of on the balcony. You know, observing the scene from the balcony. So then I have the option to join in if I want to.

MP: Okay, good. What might that look like specifically?

GILLIEN: Well, it's me being clear with my family that I'm establishing a new role. I'm not the go-to person anymore. I set boundaries around when I'm available. I'm still available, but only in a true emergency. And I'm no longer Ms. Moneybags. No more doling out cash on an as-needed basis. I'm here for sympathy and compassion and maybe getting you out of jail, but you'll have to get your bail elsewhere.

MP: So if that was your role, how would that change this Yes, But—this family obligation?

GILLIEN: It would loosen its grip, that's for sure. I could see how if I took on that role, I really might be able to leave the law and pursue work I love.

So, that's reality testing. It's not a miracle cure. Gillien still has a lot of work to do—having a difficult conversation with family members, setting boundaries, being tested, screwing up, reminding herself of her new role and getting back on the horse. And she's on her way to overcoming an obstacle that before felt insurmountable.

Each career possibility presents its own challenges, its own Yes, Buts. As you explore the possibilities, you'll make choices about whether the obstacles are real or not. Then you have to decide if you want to overcome those obstacles. If so, get started. If not, pick another possibility.

Using this approach took some of the angst out of the transition for me. Rather than beating myself up for not wanting to overcome a genuine boulder of an obstacle, I could move on. Rather than letting what someone said defeat me, I could ask myself, "Is that really true?" Sometimes it wasn't. I'd triumph over that obstacle and go on to the next one until eventually there was nothing left but my new career staring me in the face.

QUICK TIP

I highly recommend you reality test Yes, Buts with a coach or a friend. This is tough work. It's hard to be perceptive about our own obstacles; they seem like brick walls. If left to our own devices, we're more likely just to curl up in a corner. With a supportive, creative friend or coach, you'll be able to gain some perspective. You'll also have someone who will challenge you and cheer you on as you break through the obstacles.

YES, BUT HOW DO YOU GET THE JOB?

Once you start reality testing those obstacles, there will probably still be a big obstacle buzzing in your brain—how do I get the job?

A lot of dissatisfied lawyers are interested in careers that seem like a one-hundred-and-eighty-degree turn. That can be especially challenging. I've heard some rough stories—from struggling to transform your legal experience into a résumé that suits the new position, to making it to the second interview only to be told that you're too big of a risk (because you might not like the work and go back to the law), to getting zero response when you submit a résumé and cover letter. It's definitely harder now that a lot of companies are hiding behind the Internet.

I'm going to share with you a handful of time-tested, sweat-filled ideas for getting around this Yes, But. I turned to friends and colleagues who are former practicing lawyers who've been successful at getting jobs and begged them to share their secrets.

Warning: These techniques aren't the easy route. But then again, the easy route usually doesn't get you the job.

Get Some Relevant Experience

If your résumé reads like a lawyer's résumé, but you're trying to shift to, say, public relations (PR), guess what? You may not be able to get the job unless you beg, steal, or borrow some PR experience. You can only twist the phrases "document review" and "preparing memoranda" so many ways. You have to face the fact that your potential employer wants you to demonstrate at least a modicum of experience (and interest) in your new field. You need to show that you're serious.

How do you do this? Let's stay on the PR example. Join the PR organization in your town. Get involved in the projects the group is doing. Make some friends in the group. Ask if they have any additional projects they're working on or know of any that you can volunteer on. If they don't, ask them to introduce you to some other folks who can help you. Build a body of work. Basically, what you're doing is interning while you have a full-time job. Remember, I didn't say this was easy.

Or, if there isn't a local PR organization in your town, perhaps one of the local nonprofit organizations is looking for a volunteer to help promote events or the group's fundraising activities, and you can volunteer to assist them with this work.

A variation on this theme I've heard of is checking in with your law firm. Some of the nonlegal work that lawyers like to pursue is done at their firms. For example, perhaps your firm has some PR-type work going on. Ask if you can participate.

You need to build some relevant experience to show a potential employer that you are knowledgeable, and, more importantly, that you mean business about making this career change.

Create Opportunities Rather Than Seeking Defined Positions

Sometimes it's hard getting a job that's been posted. Those companies are often looking for a certain type of candidate, and a former lawyer without experience often is not it. A few of my clients have brilliantly created positions for themselves. Here's how that works. Once they're clear on the areas they want to work in, they look for small start-ups that they admire with owners they'd love to meet. (Small start-ups have more flexibility and are often owner-driven. Their owners are usually creative risk takers, so they're open to possibilities.) They track the owners down by telephone, email, or in person, depending upon the preference of the owner, and request a conversation. They do research on the companies and their founders to get a sense of how they operate. They think about how they might contribute to the companies. When they get the interview, they dazzle the founders with their knowledge of their companies, the skills they can bring to the table, and the thought they've put into crafting how they might contribute.

Start at the Bottom and Work Your Way Up to the Top

This is often one of the most effective routes to finding employment in a new career path. For example, let's say you want to be a literary agent. You could apply for the prestigious Columbia Publishing Course and then interview to be an assistant to an agent. Yes, you're working for pennies, but eventually you can join an agency as a full-fledged agent and maybe even start your own agency one day.

I also know lawyers who have joined big agencies, like William Morris Agency, and worked their way up to the top. Guess where they started? In the mailroom. It's where everybody starts.

You've Heard it Before and I'm Here to Tell it to You Again—It's Who You Know

I know, I know, you'd rather this strategy die a slow and painful death than have to hear it again, but it's not going anywhere. This one may take time. But it's not about going to a networking event and handing out a hundred business cards in thirty minutes. It's about meeting people to create connections and possibilities. You have to develop some comfort around this concept.

I can hear you complaining, "I'm not good at meeting new people," or "What if I ask for their help and they say no?" Well, there are times when we need other people to make things happen. Changing careers is one of those times. If you're trying to get a job somewhere else, you'll need someone to make you an offer. Even if you're starting your own business, you will at the very least need clients, customers, and financing. I'd love to tell you there's a way to do this by pulling yourself up by your own bootstraps, but there isn't.

Remember my interview with Debbie Goldstein, the wannabe conflict resolution consultant, in Chapter One? She was bemoaning her jobless fate to her brother. He mentioned that there was a mother at his children's school named Sheila who was in the conflict resolution business. Debbie arranged a meeting with Sheila, who warned Debbie that she only had half an hour and couldn't give Debbie a job. They met for bagels and three hours later, Sheila offered her a job. It was also for pennies and low-man-on-the-totem-pole status, but a year later Debbie had a decent salary and now she's running the show.

I'm not saying everyone you meet will fall in love with you and your witty repartee and offer you a job. But if you make the effort to find the six degrees of separation, with a little luck, you may find someone in a position to help you in your quest. And if you have a genuine interest and an overwhelming desire to be in the field and the ability to convey that, eventually you're going to come across someone who wants to take a chance on you.

THE ROADMAP

You have to have a plan. Yes, even though you haven't pinpointed exactly what you want to do yet (or even if you have), you still need a plan. In fact, because you have so many possibilities running around in your head, that's even more reason to create a roadmap.

Unless you're one of those people who can create a plan in their head and do everything on that internal list (and I'm betting you're not one of those people), you need a written plan. Let's say one of the possibilities you're exploring is starting a company that does international specialty tours, like wine and food tours in Italy and France. There's a wide gulf between Point A (practicing law) and Point B (owning a tour company). You bridge that gulf by creating a plan.

How comprehensive does the plan have to be? Well, the answer to that completely depends upon your nature. I have clients who love lists. They have a legal pad with pages and pages of things to check off. Every time they check something off this list, it's a rush. They feel virtuous.

I have some clients who would set the legal pad on fire (and possibly themselves) if asked to create page after page of things to do. The most they need is a paragraph of bullet points. Each bullet point represents a chunk of what needs to be done.

Others are more intuitive and creative. They prefer to create a *mindmap*. One way to do this is to get a big piece of poster board and draw one circle in the middle and write your new career in the circle. Draw additional circles on the rest of the poster board that contain different parts of the plan. When you're done, you'll have a big, visual representation of the roadmap.

Whatever type of plan you choose to create, I'll share a simple method that I use with my clients. You can adapt it to your needs and preferences. The roadmap consists of two questions:

1. What do you need to do?

2. Who do you need to be?

WHAT DO YOU NEED TO DO?

Let me go back to my previous example of moving from Point A, practicing law, to Point B, starting a specialty tour company. What kinds of things do you need to do? Let's create a list.

- Buy (or check out from the library) lots of books about starting a tour company.

- Save money—how much?

- Write a business plan.

- Write a marketing plan.

- Check into small business loans.

- Decide what kinds of tours you want to do and where you want to go.

- Look into partnerships—maybe you could buy out someone with experience?

- Talk to several other tour company owners, maybe spend the day with them, or even do an apprenticeship or internship.

- Look into office space. (Or can you work out of your home?)

- Check out legal and tax aspects—will you have employees?

- Discuss the career change with your parents, spouse, kids, etc.

Creating a plan, by the way, isn't about knowing with dead certainty exactly what needs to be done to move from Point A to Point B. Yes, I know we're lawyers and we like certainty, but you can't have it here. In fact, ignorance may be bliss in this situation. If you knew more about the road ahead, you might jettison the trip. Accept the fact that the road is going to be a twisty one, with lots of unexpected zigs and zags. Just remember, you can revise the map as you go. All you need now is something that can get you started.

And remember, stop waiting until you know what your one true career love is. You don't have to know what it is before you create a plan; you just need to know what possibilities excite you. And if you've done the work in Chapter One, you already have those. Don't get hung up on certainty. I know that for those of you who like certainty, this may send you over the edge, but I have to tell you, based on my experience working with people who want to change careers, it's not about being completely certain. You can wait forever trying to figure everything out. Instead, get out there, get in the mud, and get dirty.

WHO DO YOU NEED TO BE?

When I ask my clients this question, they're often puzzled. "What do you mean?" they ask. I've mentioned it already, but it obviously bears repeating. When you make a career change, it's not just about changing careers—it's about changing you.

You're changing your identity. You're shifting worlds. You can't be the same complaining, whiny, watch-television-all-Saturday person you used to be. Maybe you need to be courageous or bold or hopeful. Maybe you need to be creative, passionate, and silly. Maybe you need to be, dare I say it, a risk taker. Perhaps you need to start keeping promises to yourself instead of breaking them without a second thought. Maybe you have to start setting boundaries with loved ones so you have the time and space to achieve your dreams. You decide. Then jot down what you've discovered on your roadmap.

HARD TRUTH

Guess what the number one roadblock for my clients in making a career change is? Money? Time? Family and friends' objections? None of these.

The number one roadblock for my clients in making a career change is my clients. This is a hard realization to accept—that there's really nothing standing in the way of you making a career change except you.

When I share this hard truth during presentations, the room starts mumbling and I begin to get the distinct impression that I may be run out of town.

But it's the truth. Lawyers are very bright. We have powerful left brains. Those very same left brains that help us to perform well in the law can trap us there.

What I can tell you from working with people one-on-one is that every single one of the objections previously listed—money, time, family responsibilities, etc.—has been overcome by my clients. I've overcome some of them myself.

Spend some time with this chapter. Don't just gloss over it, shrug your shoulders, and say, yeah, well, my situation is different. Everyone has some obstacles.

Let me tell you a story. When I graduated from law school, one of my classmates decided to pursue conflict resolution work, rather than join a firm. I was happy for her but also a bit jealous. Must be nice to be married to a guy on the partnership track at a firm. If I had that kind of security, I might pursue the job of my dreams, too. About six months later, I met her for lunch. She told me the jobs were coming in, but only sporadically. She knew they'd build up eventually, but it was going to take a year or two. She said it was hard on her ego. What made it harder was her husband's attitude about it. Since she wasn't doing a substantial amount of work yet, he didn't really take her work seriously.

That's when I realized that we've all got obstacles—it's just a question of whether you want to overcome them. (My friend persevered, by the way, and now she's got a terrific, full career in the field.)

CASE STUDY
• • • • • • • • • • • •

Carolyn Pitt-Jones, age 35
Director of Business Development, Major, Lindsey & Africa, Atlanta, Ga.
2½ years in legal search
BA in Psychology, Minor: Spanish and African American Studies/Vanderbilt
*   University*
JD/American University
Years of practice: 3
Type of practice: IP Litigation, large firm in Atlanta, Ga.

What I like about Carolyn's transition is the care with which she planned her departure from a large law firm practice. Carolyn recognized and acknowledged to herself early in her career that she would not want to practice for a law firm for long. She began to explore her options, but also accepted the advice of a legal recruiter who advised her to wait a few years so that she could build her experience. Carolyn did that and continued to check out her options and to think critically and carefully about which of those options would fulfill her specific needs.

Now, please don't hear me as saying that you need to wait a few years before leaving the practice of law. That's not my point. That worked well for Carolyn. You have to make that decision for yourself based upon the career options you are exploring and your own needs. Some of the other folks interviewed for the case studies left the law after shorter periods of time. My point is that if you are just beginning to experience restlessness or just becoming aware that the practice of law is not for you, then that is the perfect time to begin planning your escape, not a few years later when you're hoping to get hit by a bus so you can get a break.

Describe what you do.

What I presently do is establish and maintain relationships with C-level [CEO, CFO, CAO, etc.] executives, most ordinarily the general counsel of corporations so that we can assess their needs in the legal department and assist them when it comes time to expand. That may include hiring their general counsel for the first time or a replacement, all the way down to their entry level people. People of all different backgrounds, but only attorneys.

Before moving to your current position, you were a legal recruiter. Describe that position.

I spent my days networking with attorneys—primarily attorneys between their 3rd and 23rd year of practice—to assess their career options, their satisfaction with current positions, and provide them with potential career options. That meant counseling, résumé drafting, assessing the marketplace, and providing them with salary information, as well as job possibilities. It also meant some business development work, staying in touch with corporations and firms to find out who and what they needed, and matching them with the candidates that I met and that my colleagues had met over time. It was for law firms, corporations, and attorneys of every stripe and level of experience.

How did you end up in legal search?

The breaking point for me for deciding that I wanted to do something other than practice law was that I was expecting my son. Once I became pregnant, I realized that in addition to not wanting to practice law forever, I wanted to have a different quality of life and a different lifestyle. I didn't want to bill 2,100–2,200 hours, which includes weekends and nights and holidays, stress, and with little time and little predictability because I was a litigator. So the tipping point was that I was going to be a mom and that I wanted to be more available for my child than I was for my managing partner. I wanted to spend more time with him than with Redwelds.

However, prior to that time I knew that I wouldn't want to practice, especially in a large law firm setting, for very long because of the same reasons—quality of life, lifestyle, and wanting to contribute and make a difference. I'm sure that's a theme that you hear from a lot of people who have left the law—they didn't feel as though they were making positive things happen for people. They were just making more money for people who were already wealthy or companies that were already wealthy, and that didn't really resonate with me as my purpose.

Interestingly enough, I knew as early as my first year [practicing law] that I wasn't going to want to stay for long, so I looked around to see what other options there might be in the city. And in the process of scouting around, I came across a legal recruiting firm and talked to the president of the company to find out what things I'd be suited for at that point, as well as later on. It was sort of an informational interview to find out how long I should do what I was doing before I could go in-house.

I thought, "Maybe I'll go in-house. I'll have a better schedule and maybe some work that's more interesting because I'd be advising business people," which I thought I'd enjoy more than practicing law in a law firm setting. Anyway, I went to speak with the president of the legal recruiting firm about a specific position, but also just to find out more about what I should do going forward to position myself. She gave me great advice and told me that I should wait and that, ordinarily, between the third and fourth years and fifth and sixth years is the sweet spot for most companies. She said, "You can switch firms if you want. I don't advise it because you're at a great firm, but for right now you should really stay the course, get knowledge, so that you have something to offer potential employers." But in addition to giving me great advice, she stayed in touch and I stayed in touch because we connected. And over time every once in a while she'd bend my ear and say, "What would you think about possibly becoming a recruiter?" And would I say, "Oh, that sounds great, but no thanks."

When all of my moons aligned—the baby was on the way, I was in a very large engagement at the firm that had me working a lot of hours, doing things not that weren't interesting but became taxing—we talked one more time, and I looked into [becoming a recruiter] with earnest one more time. It seemed to make a lot of sense with the place I was in (in my life and my career) to still be among lawyers, and a way to help lawyers who wanted to find a better career or a better lifestyle—to be a catalyst for that but not have to work those crazy hours. So I looked into it and ultimately did end up becoming a legal recruiter.

I was blessed to be able to set my own schedule and, although I was working full-time, I did it from home while watching my son, who at the time was 3 months old. When I did go into the office, I would take him with me, and a lady in the office was delighted to watch him any time we had meetings or if I had to meet a candidate. I would sometimes take phone calls in the garage or the closet and definitely while he was sleeping, but it suited me really well and gave me the flexibility that I wanted and needed to: (1) be able to be with my son; (2) still make a living; and, (3) help people, particularly those who were like me—attorneys who felt like they were not a good fit where they were—to find another opportunity that was better suited for their interests and skill set. It was cool. It was a blessing.

It was also a great opportunity because I found out that I was pretty good at doing it. It's so relationship-driven and although I didn't know it at the time, practicing, particularly in the city that I still live in, at a major firm, making friendships, connecting not only with my peers but with older and younger attorneys, with HR professionals, with anybody I actually came in contact with, came to fruition later on. Because when I left I was a rising fourth year, and, as I just said a little while ago, that's the sweet spot. So a lot of my peers were people who were looking and eligible to start going in-house. So when I started to reach out, I had a network.

By the way, I was recruited to come and do what I do now [business development], which I thought was funny. Somebody was headhunting the headhunter. I said, "You must be joking." And because I had this crazy flexible schedule I thought, "(1) you can't be serious; and, (2) you really don't want someone who works so much from home." And the fantastic internal recruiter we have said, "Don't be so sure. Let's finish our conversation. I'd love to see if there's some synergy." And there was, and I have a flexible schedule now as well [as one] that I was able to negotiate. Fortunately, that's a plus for me, and it's a plus for the company because I bring the background and experience that includes practice as well as legal recruiting.

What fears did you have about not practicing law?

One of the standard fears is purported to be—and I believe it—identity. I never had the identity concern. I think my concern initially was whether I could make a decent income. Because once you practice law, you have a level of income to which you grow accustomed, and it's tough to replace it. I was willing to take it down a few notches as a tradeoff for quality of life but my concern was—can I still make a decent living? Other than that, I can't say I had a lot of consternation about leaving the law itself. I'd done it long enough to know that it wasn't glamour and glitz. So I was okay with leaving much of it behind.

How do you define success?

I define success as making some sort of impact and being satisfied at the same time. [What that is will] differ from person to person and from time to time. For me right now, success is being able to help people while successfully making a living and being happy and good at it. It's a number of plates spinning at the same time. I think you can be successful with one plate not up in the air, but the ultimate success is to be able to have all of that going on at the same time.

How did you know that legal recruiting was the career for you?

I had talked to another couple of companies, entrepreneurs who had started similar companies in that span of time, and I found myself thinking out loud with them and realizing that I've always—as I mentioned I was a psych major—done the counseling thing as it related to my academic life, but I've also counseled friends in my personal life. I've always been the person who helped people revamp their résumés and think about jobs, possibilities, and strategies. So it just all sort of came together. If I hadn't become an attorney, it's possible I would have stumbled onto executive search anyway, but when I say the moons aligned, they really did because in addition to having that executive search proclivity already, I also had this legal background, so it all sort of came together neatly.

But I think I always had the desire to help folks and the interest in helping people with career stuff, and it manifested all at the same time in legal recruiting and now in business development.

Business development is a little different. Before, I was calling attorneys to ask them if they wanted to take a new position. Now, of course, I'm calling CEOs, GCs, and VPs of HR to ask them to give us their jobs so that our recruiters can find people for them. I've seen both sides of the house now, and fortunately the business development piece came about because of my experience as a legal recruiter, so it builds upon itself and that builds upon a legal background, having actually practiced.

What makes you different from lawyers who don't pursue their dreams?

There are fears. We touched upon some of them earlier. There's loss of identity, loss of income. Some people don't know that they have the skill set to do something other than law, particularly those who have not done anything other than practice. I had a career before I went to law school. I was an underwriter and a risk manager. So I'd been in other environments and knew that the law is not corporate America. I knew I had a skill set. So I think that makes a big difference, too. I think I didn't fear some of the top reasons that [keeps people from leaving]. I knew I could do something else.

What pressures did you experience to go the traditional route?

I never thought I'd end up at a large firm or even a firm. I just assumed I'd look into nonprofits and government positions and other things that were a creative use of my degree. But then I began to look at my amassing law school debt. It also came time to interview around second year, so I thought, "Oh, I'll interview." You kind of get caught up in the turnstile. Because once you interview and a firm or firms are interested, they offer you a summer job; so you take the summer job. And in my case I did two firms and by then you realize, "I can do this firm thing." The lure of a handsome income is there and you're already kind of committed, you're kind of invested already in doing it and you think, "Okay, I'll do it for a couple of years and I'll pay down my law school debt and segue to something else." But I think that's the part that people miss. They never segue. Either they're afraid or they forget. Somehow there's a disconnect, and I think that is why there are so many attorneys left looking like a deer in the headlights because that whole "I'll segue" thing never happens for them.

What doesn't appeal to you about practicing law?

The hours don't appeal. The sense of purpose is not fulfilling for lots of legal work. I think those are the main things.

The hours for me were larger than anything else, the time commitment. And the lack of predictability. Not having time is one thing, but not being able to predict my schedule is another. I was always having to reschedule dinner or not having dinner. Or even being able to take a vacation or go to a friend's [event]—I missed my best friend's medical school graduation because I just couldn't leave. I had a ticket and everything all scheduled, and then I couldn't come. I didn't like that.

What's the purpose of work in your life?

I'd say it's two-fold. One, clearly, is to generate income to support my family, and the other is something meaningful that enables me to develop myself. We challenge ourselves, we learn, we engage, and we hopefully get better as time goes on. We contribute in some way, whether that's time, energy, money to the community. It's an additional way to plug into the community in some way.

Anything else you want to share? A lot of lawyers express interest in pursuing legal search, like it's the Holy Grail of alternative careers.

People shouldn't think [becoming a legal recruiter] is a magic pill. They shouldn't think, "That's so simple, I must do that." Because they might not be good at it, or they might not like it, or there might be some other reason why it's not a fit. People don't understand that in order to be successful as a legal recruiter—sure, it looks easy and parts of it aren't that difficult—you have to really like talking to people. A lot. And emailing them and staying in touch with them and being persistent. And getting them to consider careers that they don't think they're suited for, only to get there and discover, "Oh my gosh, this is the best thing since sliced bread." You have to be able to help them figure out what they want to do, which, as you know, isn't always easy. A lot of it is counseling; a lot of it is holding hands.

A lot of people who seek legal recruiters are people they can't help, people who don't have a background or skill set that is marketable at that given time. Those are the ones who want it the most. And just because they need the help, I would make the extra time to do it. That's great because it's paying it forward. It also ended up working out well as a side effect, because they had friends who they'd refer who might be "placeable." But there are a lot of moving parts.

Find out about it, whether it be legal recruiting or whatever else might interest you, before you take the leap. Go on informational interviews. Do your research. Because it may look easy and it might be easy for one person, but it might be a chore for another or just downright difficult. I've seen people who've attempted to do it, who for every reason in the book should have enjoyed it and been extremely good at it, and it didn't work out for that person.

There's a level of risk in anything that we do, especially if it means change, and I think that in order to get the most reward when you make a significant change, when you go all the way out on that branch for the fruit, you just have to be as prepared as you can be before you make the leap, and know that it'll be okay either way.

• • • • • • • • • • • •

WHAT YOU SHOULD HAVE LEARNED IN THIS CHAPTER

☐ It's okay to admit defeat in the face of a particularly heinous Yes, But. It's not okay to give up your dream of finding fulfilling work.

☐ You have to have a roadmap. Where's yours?

☐ Everybody's got obstacles and everybody's sure their obstacles are the worst. It's not a competition.

chapter six

On Being Magically Transformed

LETTER FROM A DESPERATE LAWYER

Dear Monica,

Maybe this is crazy, but I thought once I figured out some career possibilities outside of the law, I'd feel different. I thought I'd be happier and more motivated. That's how I felt at first, but now it's like the honeymoon's over and I'm miserable. Instead of working on my plan to get out, I'm more interested in eating an entire package of Oreos.

Christina

Just like Christina, my clients have this fantasy that once they come up with some exciting alternative careers, they will become a different person right then and there. They will gain a never-ending supply of energy and ambition. They will never again doubt themselves. They will be magically transformed.

Actually, the title of Jon Kabat-Zinn's book, *Wherever You Go There You Are*, turns out to be a better description. My clients discover, to their great dismay, that they are the exact same bundle of contradictions after they figure out what they want to do as they were before. They have spurts of energy where they tackle every goal in sight. They have moments of weakness when they watch too much TV or go on spur-of-the-moment shopping sprees.

They have days when they are wildly enthusiastic about where they are headed and what they are going to accomplish. And then they have days where they wonder who they're kidding, and which idiot thought it would be a good idea to give up their legal career.

They're frustrated by their inability to stay at top form all the time. Actually, they feel cheated. It seems only fair that after all their efforts at finding the work of their dreams, the plan should come together magically.

I wish I had a remedy for this malady, but I don't. Who you are right now is who you will be when you figure it out. While your goals have changed, you're the same witty, bright, frustrating, lazy person you've always been.

Does that mean it's hopeless? Nope. I've got a grab bag of tools, tips, and tricks right here that you can use to get around that lovely obstacle of you! Whenever you need a little something to get you going, this is the chapter to come to.

Note: Some of these sections are short and sweet. Don't discount them—there's power in brevity, too.

GO WITH WHAT YOU'VE GOT

Know any toddlers? There are times when they are bursting with energy and times when they plop down and refuse to move another inch. Whether you want to admit it or not, you have a lot in common with a toddler. You have the same highs and lows. The difference is that most parents are wise to what their toddlers' energy levels are. You have to figure out the same thing for yourself.

Track your energy levels for a few months and write down what you discover. Are you full of energy in the mornings or maybe on the weekends? Do the weekly firm meetings sap your confidence? Or perhaps you find you're super-motivated for several weeks, and then you're not motivated to do anything but read *In Style* magazine for the next few weeks. Track it all.

And be especially vigilant about identifying the *dream-suckers*—you know, the friend or family member who means well but brings you down every time you talk to him about your dream of becoming a talk radio host.

You may find some surprises. When I did this exercise, I realized that I had low energy, enthusiasm, and faith in myself around, ahem, a certain time of the month. To my women readers, this seems obvious, doesn't it? But before I did this exercise, I found myself caught off guard by how irritable and tired I was every month, even though it was the same time every month. Brilliant.

I also discovered that as much as I loved gossiping with my friend "Carol" (definitely changed her name), she brought me way down if I ventured to talk about changing my career with her. She's a lawyer who doesn't see any point in not being a lawyer. Obviously not the go-to person for sympathy, brainstorming, or cheerleading.

Once you've identified your patterns, work with, instead of against, them. If you've got the most energy on Thursdays through Sundays, use that time to work on your roadmap. If you find you hate humanity in the morning, do your informational interviews in the afternoon. I'd suggest naptime, too, but most of my clients have trouble fitting that into their days. Plan what you will get done and what you won't the same way a parent plans around a toddler's energy levels.

SKIP THE MINUTIAE

Why is it that when we have some seriously important goals, we lose all focus? All of a sudden, it's the little stuff that's got our undivided attention. It's all the minutiae that life has to offer. Let me explain.

Your goals are grand. Your goals are *not* to look at your email as soon as you walk into your office in the morning. Nor are your goals to check off the five to ten easiest items on your to-do list. And, yet, that's the stuff that grabs your attention every single day. That's the stuff you start with, and, by the end of the day, that's the stuff that's worn you out, and you still haven't gotten to the things that really matter.

So then you think, "But that stuff has to get done." If you don't water your plants promptly, or put the dishes in the dishwasher, or handle the rest of the nitty-gritty, what will happen?

Here's a radical thought: What *will* happen if you don't do those things first? More importantly, if you don't work on your goals, what will happen?

Since I suffer from this same affliction, I decided to run a little experiment. I redirected my attention to my goals, instead of the minutiae.

What does that mean? In the morning when I walked into my office, I withstood my first impulse to check email and reviewed my goals. Instead of unpacking my luggage from a trip, I contacted a colleague to talk about a joint venture. Basically, every time I thought of something I needed to do, I resisted the urge to go do it and said out loud, "Stay on target."

Let me tell you, it wasn't easy. I work out of my home, so I uneasily watched that pile of laundry grow. And my to-do list, which is chock-full of minutiae, was luring me like the Sirens calling the sailors' ships onto the rocks.

Maybe it's not email or dishes that are the minutiae in your life. You have to figure out what is. What's the tempting little stuff that constantly gets in the way of your big, grand dreams to leave the law? For you it may be making the morning rounds at your office to chat with colleagues, or it's your insistence upon cleaning the glass table in your dining room to a sparkling shine before you begin finding your new career.

I also realize most of you have full-time jobs. Classifying your jobs as minutiae is a dangerous strategy, unless your plan is getting fired so you can collect severance. (I'd still rein that one in.) Nonetheless, I'll bet you're wasting some time there, too, that could be better spent on being efficient so you can get out and work on what really matters, like leaving the law.

WEAN YOURSELF OFF INTERNET SURFING

When I was practicing law, I firmly believed that I deserved to spend my off-time any way I felt like it. At the end of the day, I slumped on the couch in front of the TV and zoned out. On weekends I spent countless hours surfing the Web, reading and rereading my collection of mystery novels, taking marathon naps. I liked mindless activities because it seemed to me that those kinds of things helped me relax. Never mind that they weren't helping me move forward.

Judith Wright calls these types of behaviors *soft addictions*[19] in her book *There Must Be More Than This: Finding More Life, Love and Meaning by Overcoming Your Soft Addictions*. Wright defines *soft addictions* as:

> habits, compulsive behaviors, recurring moods or thought patterns. [T]hey satisfy a surface want but ignore or block the satisfaction of a deeper need. Many soft addictions involve necessary behaviors, like reading, eating, or sleeping. They become soft addictions when we overdo them and when they are used for more than their intended purpose. Soft addictions, unlike hard ones such as drugs or alcohol, are seductive in their softness. Emailing, shopping, and talking on the phone seem like perfectly harmless, pleasurable activities while we're engaged in them. When we realize how much time and energy we devote to them, however, we can see how they compromise the quality of our lives.[20]

That gave me pause. What I realized as I examined my own soft addictions, such as reading mystery novels, surfing the Web, and napping, is that they felt good in the short-term but they weren't contributing any value to my life. They're very tempting, of course, because they don't require any effort, but do they enrich my life? Not a bit. That's when I began to wean myself off those activities and focus on my own roadmap, which was definitely a high-quality activity.

I know the last thing you want to hear is that tracking your time is a good way to develop awareness of how you spend it. I can hear you now: "The main reason I want out of this profession is so that I don't have to keep a $@%* time sheet." Don't throw the book across the room just yet. You can do this exercise without actually keeping a time sheet. Just jot down approximately what you do in your spare time each day for a month or at least a couple of weeks. Although, if you really want the benefit of this exercise, keep a running tab so that you can see exactly where your hours go.

At the end of the month, grab yourself a cup of tea, sit down in a cozy chair, and take a look. Be gentle and curious—rather than harsh and judgmental—as you review the results. Ask yourself, do I have some soft addictions? What are they? What am I getting out of them? Do they nurture me? What are my deeper needs, oh, say, like having fulfilling work? What kinds of behaviors might satisfy those needs, like perhaps, working on my roadmap, and how can I begin to incorporate those behaviors into my life?

QUICK TIP

Really dreading the idea of tracking your time, since you've already got to keep a record of every dreary moment at the office? Here's a quick hint that will get you answers. Simply notice how you spend your time. Want to do some Internet surfing? Check the clock when you start and when you stop. You'll be surprised by the fact that what you thought was only "a few minutes" was actually ninety minutes.

RIDE THE WAVE

As you're making your career transition, you're going to experience a barrage of emotions—joy, excitement, passion, frustration, despair, anger. A lot of my clients don't know what to do with these deep emotions. I don't know when it started, but somehow we, the human race, have gotten out of the habit of appreciating strong emotions. Have you noticed that if you express enthusiasm or joy, you're seen as naïve or are gently (or sometimes harshly) mocked? On the other hand, a lot of us have been taught to tamp down on strong negative emotions as well—if you're feeling down, talk yourself out of it; worse yet, berate yourself if you can't snap out of it.

As a person making a transition, you're going to have to buck the current trend on this one. It's too hard to make a career change and keep your emotions in check. My advice? Allow yourself to experience whatever emotions you're having. This might sound simple, but it is often very hard to do. Here are three steps to get you going.

Note: If you're afraid of being alone with your emotions, you can do this with a friend you trust. If you feel as if there might be deeper, psychological issues at stake, maybe it makes sense to get in touch with a trusted counselor, therapist, or minister.

Step #1

Identify a place where you feel comfortable expressing strong emotions. When I'm at home, it's not a problem. Not so easy when I was at my firm. My work friends and I decided to make the cafeteria in the basement of the building our designated spot. Which leads to my next point—identify people with whom you feel comfortable sharing strong emotions. Hint: People who make snide comments when you're ecstatic or who cower when you curse are not the right ones. You need to have a place where you can go and a person with whom you can let all this stuff out.

Step #2

Identify the emotion. Resist the urge to smother it, or turn it into something else. Each of us has emotions we're comfortable expressing and emotions we're not comfortable expressing. For example, I'm not so good with being angry. I'd rather translate that emotion into being sad, which seems like a safer emotion to express to me. Get good at identifying exactly what emotion you're feeling and say it out loud, like "I am angry," or "I am giddy."

Step #3

Sit in the emotion, whatever it is. Allow yourself to actually experience it, rather than fighting it off. If you just had a particularly satisfying informational interview and you're ecstatic, allow yourself to jump up and down and shriek, instead of your usual quiet, "Well, that went well." If you're feeling angry because you feel so stuck you're not sure how you're going to make it out, throw darts at a dartboard or scream into a pillow.

VISUALIZE WHAT'S IN YOUR WAY

If you've allowed yourself to experience your emotions and you still can't get moving, there may be more at work there. (We're talking about the negative emotions here because, oddly enough, the positive ones don't stay around for long.) Often my clients just need a few minutes to go through the three-step process previously described and we can move on. Sometimes they need an afternoon or a couple of days to get past it. Other times they sense that they're letting their emotions run away with them.

Trust your instincts on this one. If you suspect that you've given the emotion enough time to run its course but you still can't get over it, it might be time to try something else. You'll need a buddy who's good at asking questions and being nonjudgmental for this exercise. What you're going to do is visualize what's getting in your way and brainstorm how you might get out of it.

Beth wants to start her own designer T-shirt business. She's had a blast creating the T-shirt designs, doing market research, even daydreaming about chic department stores and boutiques, and buying massive orders she'll have trouble filling. But lately she has been feeling stuck, and she's having trouble getting past it. So we tried this approach with her.

BETH: I just feel stuck. I've been grouching around for days now and I can't seem to snap out of it.

MP: Feeling stuck. Let's put an image to that. What does it look like?

BETH: Being stuck?

MP: Yes, if you had to create a picture, how would you describe it?

BETH: Well, it feels like I'm in quicksand, actually.

MP: Like the more you thrash about to escape, the more you get sucked in?

BETH: Exactly.

MP: So we need another way to get you out. You know that sound something makes when it's pulled out of quicksand? Kind of a *thwock*.

BETH: Sure.

MP: What will thwock you out of the quicksand?

BETH: I don't know.

Note: "I don't know" is a common refrain from my clients. That's okay if that's your response. The fact that you don't know means it's a rich question worth digging into. Just have your buddy keep exploring.

MP: That's okay. Just visualize yourself for a moment in that quicksand. You're not thrashing around, though. What would pull you out of it? Maybe someone slides a tree trunk out to you that you grab onto?

BETH: Or they throw a tire around my waist and it's attached to a steel cable that's getting pulled by a pickup truck.

MP: Okay, good. Tire around the waist, steel cable, pickup truck. Thwock. You got it? You have the image in your head?

BETH: Got it.

MP: What's the rescue truck that's going to pull you out of this quicksand?

BETH: Maybe I just need to sign up for that *solopreneur* course. I mean, the catalogue has gotten dog-eared from me looking at the course description. What am I waiting for?

MP: What *are* you waiting for? What if you sent out an announcement about your new business?

BETH: Now? I mean, I haven't left the law yet.

MP: So?

BETH: I don't have my business plan completed yet or my marketing plan or—

MP: You have designs, you have an arrangement with a manufacturing company—

BETH: And I have a way to collect orders, payments, and do shipping. I *could* send out an announcement.

MP: What else?

BETH: Some of my friends have asked me to design T-shirts for party favors. I've been putting them off, thinking I needed to have everything set up. I could do that.

We're on a roll now. We'll continue brainstorming and then Beth will have the luxury of selecting from several tantalizing options. More importantly, she's unstuck.

CLEAR OUT THE DEADWOOD

Got a lot of clutter in your life? Maybe it's blocking your ability to move on. It may be time to clear some space for your new work, for the new you. It could be as simple as clearing out your bookshelves—the ones loaded with trash novels, law school and college textbooks, your attempts to read literature, magazines, old newspapers. Or maybe your whole home needs an overhaul.

If I try to start any new project and I'm surrounded by too much stuff, my brain gets blocked as well. The same thing happens if I'm trying to start a new life. Clear out those closets, your drawers, under the bed. Throw open the windows and air the space out. Make some room for the new.

Now this tip can be a bit tricky because I have a lot of clients who like to use the excuse that they simply must do every last bit of their spring cleaning before they can get started on fulfilling their dreams. This is another one you have to trust your instincts on. Are you avoiding working on your roadmap or do you genuinely not have room for anything new in your life? If it's the latter, tackle the clutter.

GET BACK ON BALANCE

Sometimes as much as we want to focus on finding a new career, there's too much going on in our lives that we have to get around first. I'm not talking about planning a wedding or traveling to do depositions. Those are temporary things. I'm talking about major imbalances in life, such as a bad relationship (or no relationships at all), health issues—things that you haven't gotten around to fixing because you're feeling overwhelmed with everything else you have to do. I hate to be the bearer of bad news, but the feeling of being overwhelmed might not go away until you deal with the imbalance.

The good news is that you don't have to revamp your entire life. There is a simple way to pinpoint what the issues are and to come up with some small changes that have a big impact.

When you think of work/life balance, what comes to mind? For most of my clients, it's that they can only attain balance when every aspect of their lives—their work, exercising and eating well, maintaining relationships, pursuing hobbies, etc.—is in perfect alignment. Let me show you a different approach to work/life balance that's much more attainable.[21]

Step 1: Take Stock of Your Life

Draw a circle and divide it into eight pie wedges. Label each wedge with an area of your life—*money, career, physical environment* (of your home and/or your office), *personal growth, friends & family, significant other, health*, and *fun & creativity*.

Now, think about the level of satisfaction you're experiencing in each area. Are you at the center of the circle, "0" (no satisfaction), or the outer edge of the circle, "10" (total satisfaction), or somewhere in between? Draw a line in each wedge to indicate your response. If you want, you can color in the area between the new line and the center of the circle.

Here's a sample completed *Wheel of Life*.

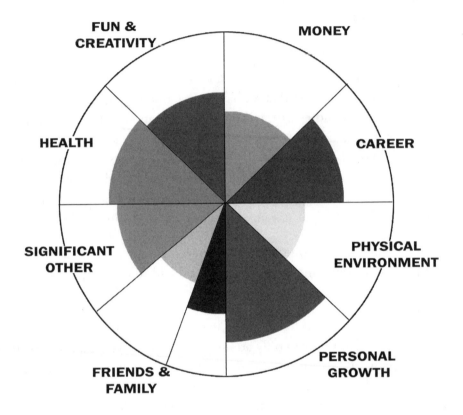

Once you've scored your level of satisfaction in each area, take a look at the new circle you created. Just imagine riding around on that wheel! A bit bumpy, isn't it?

Well, relax. The goal isn't to create a smooth wheel. Life is too short to reach for unattainable perfection. We're looking for maximum impact in a short amount of time.

Step 2: Select Which Area You Want to Focus On

How do you select the area? The simplest way is to select an area with a low score (6 or below). Or pick the one that's been bugging you the most lately. Have a 4 on "Fun & Creativity" and feel like you simply must make changes or you'll drown? Go with "Fun & Creativity."

Step 3: Answer Four Questions

You can ask yourself these questions or do this exercise with a friend. I recommend you work with a friend because you can motivate and cheer each other on.

1. What is the best possible outcome?

2. What is important to you about this?

3. What qualities do you need to bring out of yourself to accomplish this?

4. What is the first step?

Let's look at these questions one by one. They may seem simple, but the results you can experience from answering them and following through are phenomenal.

Joshua started coaching with a lot of enthusiasm. He's a seventh-year associate at a large firm in New York City who wants out of the law desperately. About three months into coaching, Joshua lost steam and couldn't get his energy back. We decided to take a look at his Wheel of Life to see what came up.

Joshua's scores were pretty high in each area except for "Health," where he scored a 3. He decides that's what he wants to focus on.

What is the best possible outcome?

> The best possible outcome? Well, it's actually more than losing weight, cutting back on cigarettes, alcohol, and fast food, and hitting the gym. I've always wanted to run the New York City Marathon. So the best possible outcome would be if I could get in good enough shape to run the marathon.

Now that's a great goal! I'm a fan of those because they'll keep you motivated. How much more motivated will Joshua be to run the marathon than with a grim goal of "lose 25 pounds or else"? Who's motivated to do that?!

What is important about this to you?

[*The answer to this one is usually more profound than you think. Joshua came up with the obvious answers first—a sense of accomplishment, feeling healthier, losing weight, etc. But as we continued to explore this question, he revealed some deeper needs.*]

My dad passed away when he was 45—that's only ten years older than I am now!—massive heart attack. He worked too hard and lived very little. I have two little girls, and I'd like to make it to see them married and to see my grandkids. I guess I'm a bit scared that I'm headed in his direction. It's partly why I want to get out of this rat race sooner rather than later.

What qualities do you need to bring out of yourself to accomplish this?

I have a one-track mind. Sure, I'm juggling ten million things, but when I'm doing one of them, I'm totally there. Like if I'm playing with my girls, we are playing. I'm not checking my Blackberry or watching the news. That laser commitment is something I need to bring to improving my level of satisfaction with my health. I don't want to be too grim about it, though. I've been told I've got a great sense of humor. So I'd like to make pursuing this goal fun, too.

What is the first step?

There's a group program for people who want to train for the marathon. I'll sign up for that so then I don't have to do it alone and there'll be some automatic structure to it. I also like the founder's attitude. He seems like a fun guy, so that'll help keep me motivated.

I like my clients to make commitments using a three-part structure:

1. what they will do;

2. when they will do it; and,

3. how I will know they've done it.

Joshua committed to signing up for the program by the end of the week and sending me an email to let me know that he had done it.

What does this have to do with leaving the law? That was Joshua's question, too. More than you think. If you're worried you're going to collapse any day and have a heart attack, leaving a widow and two young children behind, it's a bit of a challenge to focus on changing careers.

Making significant strides in one area of our lives can have a tremendous impact on other areas. Once Joshua signed up for the program, he began running regularly, cutting out the cigarettes and junk food. His sleep improved, as did his mental stamina, clarity, and mood. He also got rid of that nightmarish image that had been haunting him. All that energy, clarity, and emotional well-being he gained seeped into other areas of his life, like making a career transition.

HARD TRUTH

As if dealing with your own issues isn't enough, there are also the obstacles life and work decide to throw in your path. You're patting yourself on the back for saving a substantial sum of money, and all of a sudden your car conks out and needs major repairs. You schedule an interview, and a deposition suddenly materializes on the same day and in another city. You feel the urge to weep copiously. It can feel suspiciously like the universe is conspiring against you. Should you take that as a sign that you're not supposed to leave the law? Nope.

If you've decided to leave the law and suddenly your path is strewn with obstacles, it's a good sign. What?! Yes, a good sign.

After working with several clients and hearing the stories of other lawyers making the transition out of the law, I'm firmly convinced that chaos is a necessary part of the process of making a career transition. I see it as a test—a test of your diligence, your faith, your trust that leaving the law to pursue meaningful work is the path for you. Your job in the midst of this tornado is just to chant your mantra over and over again, "It's all a part of the process," and keep moving.

CASE STUDY

• • • • • • • • • • • •

Vivian Wexler, age 32
Assistant Director for JD Advising, Harvard Law School, Cambridge, Mass.
2 years in law school career counseling
BA in English and Political Science/University of Florida
LL.B/McGill University Faculty of Law
Years of practice: 6.5
Type of practice: corporate and financial services, large firm in Boston, Mass.

For a lot of lawyers who leave the law, there is often a precipitating event, a moment in time from which they can date their decision to leave. It can be something large and catastrophic, or something small and quiet. Vivian's precipitating event is a sad one. And, yet, without it, she's not sure she would have changed her life for the better.

It's not the event that is the key, though. The event is just the catalyst. Thinking that the precipitating event itself will transform you and your life is just wishful thinking. It's what you do after the event occurs that results in a transformation. Notice what actions Vivian takes, what big, powerful questions she asks herself—because those are the elements that help her to transform her life.

Describe what you do.

I do counseling, primarily career advising and programming for law students and alumni of Harvard Law School.

How did you get into your current career?

Fortuitously, actually. I had been practicing and had always been very, very social, and found that I would have about a three-hour attention span before I would have to go stroll and look for people to talk to. So I was very involved in lateral recruiting, lateral integration, and certainly the mentoring components that the firm needed. I was the go-to person for all of that stuff.

I had been working quite a bit and had a situation where my sister-in-law became gravely ill. I realized that I was spending an awful lot of time at the office, away from my husband at a time when he desperately needed me to be there for him. So it got me thinking. I thought to myself that this was not really a tenable thing because she is going to pass away and he is going to need me. I felt like I was in a bad situation. I wasn't very happy as a result of it because I felt like I was falling down on my job [as a wife] and on my obligations to other people in my life.

So I started thinking about alternatives and did some personality tests. Everything that I took in all the personality tests seemed to point to a counseling type of a position. I took the MBTI [*Myers-Briggs Type Indicator*], and I'm an ENFJ [*Extroverted, Intuitive, Feeling, Judging*]. [The assessments] made it very clear to me that, hey, I understand now why I need to be in a more social environment. I understand why I am constantly seeking out social interaction. I understand why the one night where I was out doing a charity event for the firm until 1:00 in the morning was the best day that I had had in months. When I came home, I couldn't go to sleep because I had so much energy. It all fell into place, it all made sense.

I started thinking to myself, what types of roles could I play for these organizations that would allow me to really have the social interaction that I need in order to be really happy in a job?

I started informational interviewing. I thought recruiting in a law firm I could do, and certainly I could do professional development. I do have some background in programming and event planning, so that's not something that would be so alien to me.

I happened to see a posting for the Harvard Law School position, and I thought to myself, hey, this seems like it would be an amazing gig to get. A friend of mine, who was the professional development [person at my firm], had done career services at Suffolk [University] Law School and coordinated the externship program at Harvard. She knew the Assistant Dean for Career Services [at Harvard]. I asked her if she wouldn't mind making an introduction so that I could go in on an informational interview, pick [the Assistant Dean's] brain about what it's like to do career services and how I could best break into the field. I was also very aware that it was very hard to move into a legal recruiting position or career services, because the positions are so heavily sought after. People really do perceive them as a lifestyle choice, and so they tend to flock to these types of positions.

[The Assistant Dean] was lovely; he was very willing to meet with me. So I came in for what was supposed to be a 20-minute informational interview, and as it turned out, we ended up talking for two hours. It became very clear early on that this would be a great job. Not only would it be a great job just to do, it would be a great job for me, and I would be particularly well-suited to do it. I did have the background and the necessary skills to be able to move into it without any sort of bridge position that would get me up to speed.

[The Assistant Dean] invited me to interview for the position. I did, and three interviews later, full-day interviews, I got the job. At that point I was terrified because if I didn't get the job, everybody at the firm knew I was interviewing because I was absent so frequently. I was really hoping that I was going to get the position because I had really put all of my eggs in one basket.

Luckily, it turned out for the best. I got my offer at the beginning of that July, and I started at the end of July. I transitioned out of the firm and was on my way. It's been an amazing transition, a very, very positive [one]. And three weeks later, my sister-in-law actually passed away, so it was none too soon.

I don't know that I would have made the transition had I not had that wake-up call. I probably would be plugging away, not miserable, but not thrilled. I never realized what it is to be in a position that you love and that you're really good at.

What fears, if any, did you have about not practicing?

I didn't have any fears about not practicing. I was concerned about the salary adjustment, because the unfortunate reality of transitioning out of practice is that you're probably not going to make the same amount of money, unless you're transitioning into an investment banking position or some sort of a business position. [*Vivian informed me that the range for career services positions nationally is between $35,000 and $55,000. Vivian started at $66,000 (Harvard Law pays more than other schools) and now makes $72,000.*] Chances are, you're going to make a hell of a lot less money, and that's a really challenging proposition for somebody, if you're the type of person who has always had the expectation that your earning potential would continue to go up and up and up. It's a major intellectual and emotional challenge to see that first paycheck that is so dramatically out of line with what you're accustomed to. Even if you have intellectualized it, you've done the math, and you know that you can make it work, and you've kind of come to the realization that this is something that you want to do, it is still a huge challenge. And that is, I think, the only thing that I miss.

People said, "You're going to miss the intellectual aspect of it." And quite frankly, for some people, that might be, but that wasn't where I got my jollies in practice. I got my jollies out of doing something awesome for the client and having that connection with the client. That was my motivation—not the work, not the intellectual exercise.

How do you define success?

I define success in the connections that you make. When you can actually connect on a personal basis with another person, know that you've helped them, and [have] been there for them. At least in my position, that is when I feel the most successful—when you realize what you are doing really does matter; you realize that you're doing it well; and, [you realize] that you're really good at it so that you don't have to work very hard to be very good at it. That's really success—when it's effortless and you're awesome.

I freely admit that I am incredibly privileged that it happened to me early, and that I have come into this. Like I said, talk about serendipity—this found me as much as I found it. We would never have anticipated when I first started practicing that this is where I would be.

That I would be working with these amazing minds, incredible students, and being able to contribute in a pretty profound way.

How did you know that this was the career for you?

I had done a lot of mentoring [at the firm]. I found that I had about six hundred nonbillable hours to mentoring and recruiting and hiring, and I realized that I was really enjoying those hours far more than I was enjoying practice.

So when I was looking for alternatives, I was looking [at] what types of positions [were] going to provide me with that sort of interpersonal interaction, with that connection that I need to motivate me.

What makes you different from lawyers who don't pursue their dreams?

A lot of it was wise planning on my part. I had the luxury of being able to make a downward adjustment because I wasn't living above my means. I never bought a crazy condo, I didn't have a car payment (I drive a used car). I lived pretty low key; I never really ratcheted up.

I do have many friends [who are unhappy practicing law], and I think what separates me from them is that it would require a huge sea change in their lifestyle. They would really need to uproot themselves dramatically in order to make the change.

I didn't have to do much of anything except spend less [per month] on my credit cards and go out maybe twice a month less. That was the big change for me.

And I needed to be conscious. I needed to budget, which I never needed to do before. But again, I was okay to do it because I had made smart choices.

I think that that is the fundamental, biggest barrier to change. People don't think that they can [change] their lifestyle because they've gotten accustomed to a lifestyle that is a six-figure-a-year lifestyle, and a lot of these jobs are not paying that.

What pressures, if any, did you experience to continue practicing?

[I was] pretty lucky because when I told my parents, my mother said, "Finally. You finally figured it out. I'm so glad you came to the decision yourself. I didn't want to say anything." I told my husband, and aside from crunching the numbers, he was also [very happy.]

I never realized, and I didn't realize until then, how hard it is [for family members when their loved ones practice law]. For a lot of people, law firm practice is an amazing, intellectually satisfying, fulfilling, exciting [thing], but you need to have buy-in from every single person in your family.

What doesn't appeal to you about practicing law?

You're by yourself an awful lot. I mean, I am a bit of an anomaly because not everybody would find that particularly offensive. Myself, I know that I work better with other people. I am highly social, so for me, I have maybe two hours to where I can be by myself, and then I get really lonely.

At the firm, it was funny because I would always have people in my office just talking. They would be talking, I would be working, but I would have a "coffee klatch" in my office. I had dim lighting and a fountain. The partners would come by and take their shoes off and come and give me projects. I mean, it really was very funny, but it just goes to show you, right? There are just people who are not meant to be behind a closed door.

I am not meant to be that person behind a closed door. Here, I have students in and out of my office all day long.

What's the purpose of work in your life?

Well, if you would have asked me that two years ago, it would have been very different. I have to pay the bills, but I think now [work is] a social outlet. Before, it was truly, specifically to pay the bills. Now it is much more of a social outlet.

Here, this is where I can really [be myself]—I have a bobblehead dog that I use to tell the students' fortunes. I ask the bobblehead dog, "Bobblehead Dog, is this one going to get a job for the summer?" And the bobblehead dog nods yes. I mean, this is like the stuff, it's the shtick. And that's the stuff that makes it fun—for me, anyway.

[Students] love it, they eat it up. And talk about success—that's when you feel like you're successful. When [students] come in, they're so nervous [about finding jobs]. But then when they leave, they're dying [laughing] because bobblehead dog just told them they're going to get a job. That is success, you know? It's a question of how you measure it, and for me, it's when they call me after they graduate to tell me that they got engaged. Or, they call me when they get straight As.

That's a pretty profound thing: someone, a stranger, whose office they fall into. Then all of a sudden they are just stopping by to hang out and talk to you about what is happening in their classes. That's when you know that you're successful.

You do know that every lawyer wants to be in career services at a law school and thinks it's another one of those Holy Grail alternative careers, like legal recruiting.

For some it is, and for some it's not. [For example,] legal recruiting is a primarily sales-based business. People don't realize how much sales they're going to be doing, and so it's not right for everybody.

Career services is not right for everybody, either. I think that you really need to be genuinely interested in connecting with students and have empathy for what to you [may seem] trivial. Especially at some of the top tier schools, you know these students don't have anything to worry about. [They'll get jobs.] Their worries, fears, and concerns—they're going to be fine, and you know they're going to be fine. You've really got to have a lot of patience.

Also, there is a huge component of programming, so you need to be pretty adept [at that], [paying] attention to detail and logistics. Creativity is also important.

Anything else?

You can change careers. You can do it. It's going to require an adjustment. It's going to require a realignment of your priorities, your financial priorities mostly, but also, your understanding about what success is. Because up until now you think that being in a law firm, being a lawyer is the pinnacle of success. And what is interesting is, I've found that people are far more impressed that I am doing this position at Harvard Law School than they ever were when I used to say that I was a corporate lawyer.

I have much more credibility. I'm making a lot less, but I've got much more gravitas being an assistant director at Harvard Law School then I ever did being "Joe Schmoe, Corporate Lawyer."

It's a question of realigning what your idea of success is and your idea of attaining success in your professional life. And if you're able to make those adjustments—the financial adjustments and [adjusting to] the idea of what being successful means—then it is incredibly doable.

It's also incredibly worth it, because what they say is true: money does not buy happiness. And you've got to look at your compensation, because I think that money is really the biggest sticking point for a lot of people. People cannot wrap their heads around the fact that they are going to be making so much less than they're currently making. But, when you look at it, what you're being paid [as a lawyer], it's hazard pay. You're working two jobs in most of these law firms. When you take that whole component out of your life, it's amazing what these [alternative career salary] packages can offer you. More vacation time, being able to take your vacation time, all of that is worth money. So the monetized value of your time is so powerful when you actually look at it, that it's not such a stretch. And if you can get okay with it, then it is absolutely doable, and it's worth it.

● ● ● ● ● ● ● ● ● ● ● ●

WHAT YOU SHOULD HAVE LEARNED IN THIS CHAPTER

☐ Who you are *before* you figure out what you want to do is who you'll be *after* you figure out what you want to do. The trick is learning how to work with you.

☐ It's not about being perfect and getting rid of all the soft addictions in your life. It's about balancing more on the side of spending your time creating a life and work that will bring you joy, peace, meaning, and fulfillment.

☐ Addressing other aspects of your life, like your health and your relationships, will help you gain traction in this career adventure.

chapter seven

When the Thought of Letting Go of that Six-Figure Salary Is too Daunting and How to Get Around Whatever Else Is Getting in the Way

---

LETTER FROM A DESPERATE LAWYER

Dear Monica,

This is probably a question you hear all the time. I just want a list of the other six-figure jobs out there. Can you give me that?

Neil

LETTER FROM A DESPERATE LAWYER

Dear Monica,

I don't mind taking a pay cut, but there are some things I'm not willing to give up. I'm not giving up my house, my car, my wardrobe, my vacations, my daily frappuccino…

Tia

Money. We have to get into this issue and get into it thoroughly or your fears about not having it are going to continue to hold you in their grip.

Is it crazy to give up a six-figure salary? This chapter is where we sort out what you're willing to give up in order to have fulfilling work (and what you're not).

JUST ENOUGH

I'm going to say something controversial here. I suspect that most of you, if not *all* of you, do not have to have that six-figure salary. You want to have it, you'd like to have it, but do you absolutely have to have it? Probably not.

Hang in there with me. I'm not suggesting that you shouldn't pursue a $100K+ income if you leave the law. If it's important to you, you should pursue it. And the inability to make that kind of money the minute you're out of the starting gate shouldn't preclude you from making your great escape from the law.

So here's my theory on this one—I've always had the sneaking suspicion that being filthy rich, while sounding immensely attractive, has its own set of problems. As does being poor—obviously. When I left the law, it seemed to me then that what I needed was just enough money.

What constitutes *just enough*? Obviously, it varies by person, but I would define it as a sufficient amount to take care of all my needs and the little luxuries. A sufficient amount so that I don't have to worry about whether I will be able to pay my bills or take care of unexpected emergency expenses. Enough to set some aside for retirement as well.

Nothing I'm going to say here is unique or rocket science. But it has to be said because, for some reason, lawyers who want out have a tremendous amount of trouble comprehending this concept. Your Gremlin (the same one that tells you you're crazy for contemplating leaving the law) gets especially active in this area.

If we use this measure of just enough, first you have to figure out exactly how much is enough. I actually think the best time to play with this question is while you're still earning that fat salary. You can test out whether having less income is feasible with the cushion of your current salary. Again, that's not to say you won't earn a large salary if you leave the law, but I can guarantee you there is no greater sense of freedom than when you figure out you don't have to have that salary.

The first step is clearing the decks. Money, how much you have, and how you manage it, can get confusing very quickly. It's not just the actual numbers—it's the emotions that swirl around it. First I want you to get some cold, hard clarity—figure out your debt levels, savings, and budget—so you can get past whatever demons you've got in your head. My clients like to hide when we get to this part of coaching. It feels like not knowing is better than knowing. What they discover—and what you'll discover—is that clarity, no matter how scary the results (and they're not always scary), is a relief. You finally know where you stand. And what you have to do to get where you want to be.

HOW MUCH DEBT DO YOU HAVE?

Don't think about your law school debt just yet. I'm talking about what's known as *bad debt*. Yes, those credit cards. My mantra for years was, "Charge it!" I wasn't excessive in my charging, but I was using my credit cards as a crutch. I figured as long as I was able to pay the minimum balance, what's the big deal? When I realized how much money I was spending in paying interest and the ridiculous fact that I couldn't even remember what I'd bought with the card, I decided it was time to come up with a new approach.

The first step for me then was coming up with a plan to pay off this debt as quickly as possible. Those interest charges were a real incentive—it got on my nerves when I saw how much they were costing me.

The second step was to commit to only charging what I could afford to pay off each month. If I couldn't pay it off that month, I couldn't put it on the card.

How much debt are you carrying around?

SHOULD YOU PAY OFF YOUR LAW SCHOOL DEBT?

I don't have the definitive answer on this one. You have to decide what's best for you. I always thought that paying off my law school debt was a worthwhile goal, but I had a lot of debt (more than $100K). When I calculated how long it would take me to pay off my debt, I cried. I was going to be at the firm a long while unless I wanted to live in a hovel and eat ramen noodles for every meal.

I decided a better approach for me was to pay down my law school debt a certain amount so that what was left would be manageable, as long as I had a reasonable income coming in.

Some of my more dedicated classmates have been able to pay off their law school debt. But be careful. Some of those same classmates swore up and down they were leaving the minute they sent off that last payment and they're still at their firms. They found they'd grown accustomed to the lifestyle those big paychecks afforded them.

HOW ARE THOSE SAVINGS COMING?

I always thought saving money was a good idea in theory. But by the time I got to the end of the month there was no money left—or very little, anyway. If you haven't heard of *pay yourself first*, get ready to become familiar with a brilliant concept. Instead of waiting to see what you'll have at the end of the month, earmark a certain amount to pay to yourself when you receive your paycheck and then do it—without fail.

You have to make some choices about where to park it—savings account, money market account, etc.

Warning: Don't spend too much time figuring out where to put it. It's another little trick your Gremlin likes to play on you. It says soothing, seductive things like, "It's important to get this right." Next thing you know, six months have passed and you've got zero saved nowhere. It's more important to set an account up and get the funds rolling in. You can always change accounts later.

If you're not trustworthy, set it up as an automatic debit. They're already taking health insurance, parking, etc., out of your paycheck, so believe me, this is not a new concept.

SHOULDN'T YOU BE SAVING FOR RETIREMENT?

This is a really touchy question. Granted, I don't want to be working because I have to until I'm on my deathbed.

On the other hand, it was an important enough trade-off to me to get my freedom first. So I focused on saving—so I'd have a cushion as I started my business—rather than putting money into my retirement account. Now that I'm doing work I love, I'm rebuilding my income *and* my retirement account.

THAT NASTY SIX-LETTER WORD—BUDGET

Nobody wants to hear it, but you have to get a grip on this one. You have to find out how much money is going out of your pocket. It's the only way to determine how much money you *want* to go out of your pocket.

I always hated when financial books advised creating a budget. *How?* Sure, the major categories are obvious—I knew how much I spent for my mortgage, electricity, Internet service, etc. But those weren't the problem areas. It was all the discretionary spending. Setting arbitrary limits wasn't going to help. I'd tried that in the past and ended up feeling deprived, which usually led to blow-out spending sprees. I needed to know how to figure out what was reasonable for me.

Rather than make changes, I decided just to track my expenses first. How meticulous you are about this is up to you

When I decided to keep track of my expenses, I went my own obsessive-compulsive route. I put an envelope and a little notebook in my purse. The envelope was for all receipts and the notebook was for any expenses for which I didn't have a receipt.

I kept track of every expense that way for three months. Then I created categories and calculated totals.

I did not like what I was seeing. It turns out I'm a bit of an impulse shopper. I'd go to the bookstore and drop $50–$75 easily. Wanting a new lipstick? I'd end up buying a whole new face at the Bobbi Brown makeup counter. Feeling like I had nothing to wear? I'd try to reinvent my wardrobe—including shoes—at retail price.

So I decided to experiment. What if I set aside a specific amount of dollars for clothes shopping, a specific amount for eating out, etc., for the month and see if I could live with that? If not, I'd adjust it. I experimented with totals for the next several months. Then I created a budget—a budget based on how I actually lived and with reasonable aspirations.

QUICK TIP

Make use of technology. If you haven't already signed up for online banking, do so immediately. If you're mainly using your debit card and credit cards to make purchases, you've got easy-to-use resources on the Internet that track all your income and expenditures.

STAY WITH ME

As you can see, this stuff takes some time and some serious fortitude. What helped me stay focused was the vision of that better life I was going to have once I left the law. Remember the *Ideal Day* exercise you completed earlier? If you haven't already posted your *Ideal Day*, do it now. Meditate on it every day. Set aside some time to daydream those big beautiful dreams you have. Let them give you energy and joy.

Once you wipe out your credit card debt, pay down (or off) your law school debt, and create a reasonable budget, celebrate! That is no small feat—it is a *major* accomplishment. It's much easier to play ignorant, to buy everything your miserable heart desires, than to shine a hard, cold light on your spending habits and quirks.

Now it's also time to have some fun. You're ready to play the *What If? Game.*

THE WHAT IF? GAME

This is where you get to speculate about what just enough might be for you. This may be the most liberating game you will ever play in your life. It was for me.

A few years ago I flirted with the idea of joining a career services office at a law school. I interviewed for the position and got salary information. Boy, did that salary look low compared to my law firm job. I was uneasy, thinking, "I'll never be able to survive on this salary." But I pulled out my budget, thought about what adjustments I'd need to make, and played around with the numbers. The law school was in another state, so I did some additional cost of living research. Then I crunched the numbers and crossed my fingers. To my shock and delight, I realized I could actually live on this salary.

That's not the only part of the What If? Game, though. You are looking at trade-offs. Remember, early on, when I asked you in Chapter One what you were willing to give up? I'd always thought I'd be willing to give up a portion of my salary but *only* if I'd be getting something very valuable in return—job satisfaction.

I knew that getting up and going to my law firm job was very hard for me. I knew I was having migraines and stomach problems because I didn't like my job. I knew that I spent my weekends miserable, especially Sundays, as I counted down the hours until I had to be back in the office. And forget about those weekends when I worked!

I thought, what if this job is a perfect fit for me? What if I'm using my talents, I'm surrounded by folks who love what they do, and I'm making a difference? Would that be worth the decrease in income? I decided that it would be.

It was liberating. That six-figure salary no longer had its grip on me.

The other massive realization was that if I traded dollars for job satisfaction, I wouldn't need to impulse spend anymore. A lot of my spending—a last-minute trip to the Bahamas, my smoothie every morning, the expensive massage—was my way of relieving the pressure of having to go through this career ordeal. If I had to have this job, then I simply had to have a reward. Several costly rewards, in fact.

I slowly came to the realization that if I had work I loved, I wouldn't need so many rewards. The work itself would be the reward.

THE SECRET OF COURAGE: SIX WAYS TO BRING OUT YOUR INNER SUPERHERO

Okay, we've tackled the money obstacle. One of the other biggies I mentioned earlier is fear. Big, stinking fear. Leaving the law requires courage like nothing else. How do you tap into it?

At a function, a colleague asked me what I did for a living. I explained that I'd recently left the practice of law to start a coaching business. He said, "That must have taken some courage." I said, "Thank you," but scoffed to myself, "You're no superhero."

A few days after the function, it hit me. I am courageous, and so are you. I began to think of all the fears my partners-in-crime in leaving the law have plowed through to get to this point and all the fears we continue to face now. And, yet, we persevere.

How do we do it? Here are six steps to help you tap into your inner superhero.

Step 1: Listen to the Whispers

What are your secret fantasies? "I'd love to own a bead store," you say. Or, "I'd really like to write." Or maybe your inner voice isn't so specific, but it says, "I hate what I'm doing. It's so hard getting up every morning. I want so much to enjoy my work." Rather than belittling or ignoring your fantasies, nurture them. Ask a bead store owner if you can spend a day at her shop. Join a writers' group. Sign up for a new and outrageous class.

Step 2: Build a Bridge

When my clients first think about leaving the law to do something else, all they can see is the abyss between their current life and their future. They have to nail one board to another to create a path. First, they explore a possibility by reading about it; talking to others in the profession; signing up for a course, maybe. They are living proof that those nailed boards build and build until, to your astonishment, you've built a bridge and you can walk over to the other side.

Step 3: Invite Fear in for a Chat

The more we try to ignore our fear, the more it gnaws at us. Sit in a comfortable chair and actually think about your fears. Whenever I do this, I can overcome my fears—or at least take away the power they have over me—in just a few minutes.

Step 4: Give Some Lucky Person the Privilege of Helping You

If, in spite of my advice to surround yourself with helpful friends, a support group, and the buddy system, you're still trying to go it alone, get over it. I admit I also used to be a big proponent of the I-can-do-it-all-by myself system. What if I ask for help and the person says no? Worse yet, what if she laughs? I've found that, in the real world, if someone can help me, she does it willingly and gladly.

Step 5: Bring Back the Gold Star Stickers

Remember those stickers you got for good behavior in second grade? It's so easy to forget you've made progress. Keep track of what you've done so you'll know how far you've come. One of my clients was frustrated recently by her so-called lack of progress. So I advised her to take out a piece of paper and write down absolutely everything she'd done up to date. When she saw how much she'd accomplished, she was pleased with herself.

Step 6: Give Yourself a Treat

When a child gets an A on a test, what parent says, "We'll wait and see what grade you get for the semester"? None. So why do you refuse to acknowledge your own progress? Reward yourself every time you take a baby step. Create a list of rewards and let them motivate you to take more action.

We tend to define *courage* as doing something big and outrageous—plunging into a burning building to rescue a child; saving a planet from destruction; or, even rushing into our boss's office today and announcing, "I quit!" and starting our new venture tomorrow.

The big secret is that courage is actually something much more attainable. Merriam-Webster's definition of *courage* is simply: "mental or moral strength to venture, persevere, and withstand danger, fear, or difficulty." Not a single reference to "leaping tall buildings in a single bound."

READY TO DEFINE SUCCESS FOR YOURSELF, RATHER THAN LETTING EVERYONE ELSE TELL YOU WHAT IT IS?

We're not even aware of it, but most of us are driven by what everyone else tells us we want. Society tells us we want the windowed office, the luxury car, and the big house. Even my clients who pride themselves on their ability to ignore societal pressures are often ruled by what their loved ones want for them. Sure, your family and friends have your best interests at heart—they love you!—but they've decided what your best interests are.

Heard any of these comments before?

- "I don't understand. What more do you want?!"

- "You need to learn to adjust your expectations about work."

- "Let me tell you what you should do…"

- "You went to law school and now you don't want to be a lawyer?!"

Most of us get so caught up in what everyone else thinks that we feel we have to get their permission to make a career change. "If only I could get my dad to understand how unhappy I am," wails Liza, an in-house attorney. Liza is so miserable she's starting to experience physical symptoms—stomach problems, migraines. Her body is trying to grant her the permission that her mind refuses to give her.

You're going to be fighting an uphill battle throughout this book if you can't give yourself permission—permission to consider leaving the law, permission to dream up possibilities and explore them, permission to leave to do work that brings you joy.

WHAT WILL IT TAKE FOR YOU TO GIVE YOURSELF PERMISSION?

For some of us, it's as simple as acknowledging that we're scared. As one client with a highly developed imagination (and sense of humor) confided in me, "I'm afraid if I try to pursue what I want, I'll end up in the subway wearing a *Flashdance*-style Harvard Law sweatshirt pandering for change."

For others, it's the realization that we can't sit at our desks, day after day, and count on the prestige, security, and salary. We need something more, even if that means disappointing our family and friends. I'll let you in on a little secret. When you leave the law and pursue work that fulfills you and pays the bills, your family and friends will be thrilled. "You're like a different person!" my clients' loved ones exclaim once they've made the leap. You may even find some of the people who gave you the hardest time are now nodding their heads and saying, "We knew it was time for you to leave. We could tell how unhappy you were."

HARD TRUTH

What do you want? To spend your life pursuing everyone else's dreams for you? Or to take a step outside this self-imposed box and make a mad dash for living your own glorious dreams?

CASE STUDY

• • • • • • • • • • •

Victoria Sanders, age 47

Literary Agent, Managing Owner, Victoria Sanders & Associates LLC, New York, N.Y.

17 years in publishing

BFA in Drama/New York University

JD/Benjamin N. Cardozo School of Law

Years of practice: 0

Victoria has a line in her interview that has stuck with me. She said, "I didn't give myself an option not to succeed." That's serious stuff.

What if you couldn't—wouldn't—allow yourself to fail at pursuing work you love, whether it's getting a new job or starting your own business? Take a minute and imagine what it would be like not to give yourself the option of failing.

What would that give you? I imagine it would give you focus, clarity, a strong sense of purpose, and conviction. Maybe even some courage. That's what Victoria has, and that's what I want for you.

Describe what you do.

At its core, I am an advocate for authors. My job is to not only help writers develop their projects to be the best that they can be, but to help them sell their work into any and all territories and exploit all ancillary rights. I am an editor, salesperson, marketer, and mommy.

How did you end up in this career?

Here's the scoop. I grew up in the entertainment business. I lived in Hollywood. I always knew I was going to be in the entertainment business in some capacity. I thought I was going to be in the movie business because my father, uncle, and whole family were in the movie business.

When I was still in law school, I thought I was going to take that law degree, become an entertainment lawyer, then eventually become a movie producer.

While I was in law school, I had a wonderful entertainment law professor named Eric Rayman. Eric invited me to clerk at Simon & Schuster. I had always been a voracious reader, so going into a publishing house was pretty glamorous, plus it was the publishing house of Richard Simon, who was legendary.

I was a law clerk for a little less than two years before I graduated law school. [Simon and Schuster] offered me a job when I graduated as Director of Contracts and Copyrights. I took it.

I had interviewed with some law firms as well, but I was never really interested in practicing law to the extent that I wanted to be a litigator or get that involved in the law per se. I was always really interested in the deal. I liked the business side. I have always liked the business side of the movie business and the publishing business.

I went to Simon & Schuster and worked there a couple of years. Then I realized I really didn't like Corporate America because Simon & Schuster was a very corporate company. I slowly came to the realization that I should give agenting a try.

The irony of all this is that my father passed away while I was still in law school in my last year. When I was a little girl, my father said, "Kid, you should either be a lawyer or an agent." He told me this from 10 on. I have no idea why he said that, but to say to a 10-year-old, "You should be a lawyer or an agent, kid," is kind of funny.

Then, of course, I went and did both after the old man passed. For whatever reason, he saw in me the ability to talk a good game. You need an entrepreneurial drive to be a successful agent.

I left Simon & Schuster to work for Carol Mann at her agency for a little less than a year. After Carol, I went for only four or five months to work with an agent named Charlotte Sheedy.

After about a year and a half total of working for these two agents, I decided I was the type of personality that needed to work for myself. I am way too stubborn to be told by other people what to do. That's held me in good stead in building my own agency.

I'm very self-motivated. I talked to my partner in life. We agreed that I should give it a shot. I had to do a little business plan because she's a corporate lawyer and she said you have to plan out your business strategy. In February of '93, I opened up the agency.

It normally takes people five to seven years to make a profit. I did it in about three. I got lucky. My first novelist was Connie Briscoe. She hit the *New York Times* Best Sellers list with her second book, *Big Girls Don't Cry*. It's been phenomenal ever since.

It's a job, and jobs are hard some days. I love my job because, having grown up in the movie business with a lot of people in my family who have been writers as well as directors and producers, I know that writers are the people who get shat upon the most. They're the ones who need the most protection.

I like nothing better than taking somebody who is incredibly talented and shepherding them through the business to help them become what they want to be and make a living doing what they want to do. I like to be the person standing behind them, making sure they don't get screwed. It floats my boat.

What fears, if any, did you have about not practicing law?

Honestly, none. The majority of people I went to law school with didn't enjoy practicing law. They knew it pretty quickly.

You have to understand that I also was privileged because my partner, Diane, was on the law review. She went right into a major firm.

I saw her coming home at 2:00 a.m., 3:00 a.m., 4:00 a.m., or 5:00 a.m. in our first year that she was working. Once she didn't come home for three days. I had to send shirts and stockings down to her at the firm. I thought, "You have to be kidding me. That's not human."

I have no regrets about not practicing law. I'll be honest with you that it helped that I didn't have an option. I took the bar and didn't pass it. My father had just died. What can I say? It wasn't my thing.

I will never forget it. When we were in law school, Diane, who did so well while I just did okay, kept saying, "When we go into these exams and the professor asks what you think, they're lying. They want to know what they think. They don't want you to actually have an original thought process." I said, "Why are they asking me what I think?" She said, "They just say that. Don't pay attention to that."

When I went in to take my final exams in my third year, which was my last year of law school, my father had died just the week before. I remember going to those exams and thinking, "I don't give a [crap] about you. I don't give a [crap] about this school. You can all drop dead for all I care."

I walked into that exam and thought, "Let me try her theory." I regurgitated everything and got straight As. I should have listened to her, right? For the last twenty-one years, I've been trying to make it up to her. I listen to everything now.

It was a really good education for me in terms of my business. You have to be certain of what people want from you. Sometimes they say they want X, but they really want Y. There's a lot of intuitive and emotional intelligence that goes into being a successful businessperson.

How do you define success?

For me, success is looking up at the main wall in my office and seeing an 11-foot by 11-foot wall covered in books that I've helped shepherd to publication by people I respect. I look at that wall and take my obligation to these writers very seriously.

That wall not only represents them, their lives, and their art, but it also represents them being able to pay their bills, put their kids through school, and survive. That's success to me. I make a living, and they make a living. We're doing something that has some value.

We're not curing cancer. I wish we were. But in terms of what I do, I try to do it every day the best I can and represent the people as aggressively and fairly as I can. It's very much like a calling. I know it sounds hackney, but it's true.

How did you know that this was the career for you?

I didn't. I hoped that agenting would be for me.

As I said, my father had passed the year before. He had been a two-time Academy Award–winning director and had loved his work. I didn't know what to do. I'd been a big reader my whole life. I knew I loved the entertainment business. I knew I didn't want to be in the movie business, so I hoped.

I didn't give myself an option not to succeed. Like many people who have had success in their fields to whatever degree, I just looked upon my situation and said, "I can't fail. It's not going to happen." That's the way I approached this.

Do you remember once it began to click? Was there an "aha moment?"

I don't think I've had an "aha moment," per se. I have moments, like anybody, where I think, "This is working. I've succeeded in this." In order to be good, every day, you have to be worried that you're not good enough. That's what drives me.

I don't think I've had a moment where I've thought, "I'm all that and a bag of chips!" Frankly, I don't want it. You have that moment then you get sloppy. I could just be neurotic.

What makes you different from lawyers who don't pursue their dreams?

I'm very lucky. I had the ability to pursue this because I had a supportive partner and family. You can't get enough positive reinforcement from the people who love you, your teachers, and the people you work for, provided you're doing a good job. That's always held me in good stead.

I've had wonderful agent mentors, who are phenomenal people I'm still friends with to this day. I, in turn, endeavor to mentor younger agents because it's important to try to educate people to come up in the agenting business and have a good work ethic, morals, and character. Those are important qualities.

You mentioned that you didn't like practicing law. What doesn't appeal to you about practicing?

This is a lousy phrase, but lawyers are, for the most part, deal breakers, not deal makers. There are very few lawyers who have a business sensibility. They're always looking for what's not going to work. It's a glass-half-empty thing.

What's the purpose of work in your life?

It gives you confidence. I'd go mad without it. I get excited. It's like anything. There are good days and bad. It's a thrilling thing to read a manuscript or work with a client for years to help them every year to do a book. It's always new. That's the big thing. You never know what the day is going to bring. That can be fun.

Anything else?

Like anything, if you're lucky, you have to figure out what floats your boat. What excites you?

I knew a woman who was a corporate executive out of Chicago. Her area of expertise was diversity marketing. It was fine and everything, but she didn't love it. What she loved to do was bake.

She started a pound cake company. She ships pound cakes all over the country. She has contracts with some of the major airline carriers now. Who knew? You bake something, and the next thing you know, you're running a corporation. That's what she liked to do.

Find your thing. As early as I can remember, my nose was always in a book to the extent that the nickname my brother gave me as a little girl was "Dilly" because he associated my constant reading and my eyes traveling over the pages.

I love what I do. I'm always reading magazines, newspapers, and books. That's my thing. What else am I going to do? I'm not good for anything else.

• • • • • • • • • • • •

WHAT YOU SHOULD HAVE LEARNED IN THIS CHAPTER

☐ Until you figure out how much money is just enough, money will hold you in its grip.

☐ What if you traded dollars for career satisfaction? What would that be like? (I'm not telling you that you should do that. I'm asking you to think about what that would be like.)

☐ Letting other people define success for you robs you of your freedom to create the life you want for yourself.

chapter eight

Dipping Your Toe in the Icy, Shark-Infested Waters

LETTER FROM A DESPERATE LAWYER

Dear Monica,

I'm beginning to feel like a loser. I've always wanted to be a painter. At least I thought so. I tried it out as a recreational activity and it feels too isolating. Then I got all excited about owning a mystery bookstore. But when I interviewed a bookstore owner, I realized that all of the details would drive me crazy. I'd just prefer to read mystery novels. Now I'm thinking about starting a film festival in my town. Is it crazy that I'm all over the map?

Carmen

Wouldn't it be awesome if you could march into a partner's office, drop your letter of resignation on the desk, and flounce out? Today? But rather than giving into the urge, why not dip your toe in the water to see how it really feels? Because if you're anything like my clients, as good as that fantasy feels, you're scared to death. No matter how miserable you are practicing law, at least it's familiar. Leaving the law can feel like crossing an icy cold ocean complete with snapping sharks. I promise you, the water's warm (and there are no sharks in sight). But the best way to find that out—and I realize it's not as glamorous as shouting, "I quit!"—is following the roadmap you created and being flexible when the roadmap isn't working.

FOLLOWING THE ROADMAP

What's happening with the roadmap you created back in Chapter Five? Did you spit out one idea after another with reckless abandon and now the plan is languishing in your desk drawer? Get it out, blow the dust off, and let's get started.

And lest you've forgotten, let me remind you about "it." Remember "it," your one true career love that you're pining to find? I told you in no uncertain terms in Chapter Five to stop obsessing about what "it" is and just get started. Let me say it again. You don't have to know what "it" is because even if you did, "it" is probably going to evolve as you get out there and work your roadmap. You may end up somewhere you never dreamed of being. Rather than just telling you about this phenomenon, I want to show you what happens as you create and follow your own roadmap.

I'm going to use my own experience of working with my roadmap in this section. I realize most of you aren't necessarily interested in the careers I explored. I'm using my own journey because it is too abstract to talk about this concept without a personal example. I'm also doing it this way because I want to show you how crazy a roadmap can look. Lawyers often assume that making a change could be a nice, neat process if only they could figure out the key. In reality, it's not straightforward.

Don't get caught up in (or bored by) the specifics of my career exploration process. Notice the ups and downs, the zigs and zags, the great leaps forward, and the stuttering steps backward, because all of that is what you'll experience as you work your own roadmap.

Ever heard of the now-defunct Disney World ride *Mr. Toad's Wild Ride*? Even if you haven't, I'm sure you've got an image in mind based on the name of the ride itself. That's what following my roadmap was like. Strap on your seat belt.

MY OWN WILD RIDE

Note: The italics in the following section represent my thoughts as I went through the roadmap process.

Here's the short list of career possibilities that appealed to me: coach, interior designer, image consultant, director of career services at a law school, trainer/consultant, and lawyer in another practice of law.

Coach. Discovered the coaching profession in a book, *Life Makeovers: 52 Practical & Inspiring Ways to Improve Your Life One Week at a Time* by Cheryl Richardson, and was ecstatic. *I've been coaching people all my life! This is a profession? I could become a life coach!* Went online and did a full onslaught of surfing to find every possible article, comment, and forum on the coaching profession. Lots of books about coaching were coming out at the time. Bought and devoured them all. Was excited as a whole new world blossomed in front of me.

The doubts seeped in. *But where's the prestige? This is such a new thing. I'm going to leave the practice of law to become a life coach? How hokey would that be?! Forget it. Ooh—interior design. I love closets, bathrooms, and home offices. Maybe I could specialize in those.*

Interior designer. Fell in love with interior design TV show where the designer helps warring couples find ways to bring both their ideas into the design. *That's a combination of interior design and conflict resolution. I have a background in conflict resolution so maybe that wouldn't be such a weird shift.* Sent the TV show designer an email and he replied with kind words of encouragement but explained it's a tough field. Read lots of books. Did a few informational interviews with some local interior designers. *There's a distinction between interior designer and decorator. I could be a decorator right now, but I'd have to go back to school and get a license to be an interior designer. I'm not sure I like the idea of doing something that's not credentialed. That feels hokey. But school? That's more money and it's not like I'd want to start out on my own right after I graduated. I'd probably want to work for someone for a few years. Be an employee? Yuck.*

Visited a California Closets store. Made an appointment with a consultant to take a look at my closet. Picked her brain on the sly while she was taking a look at my mess. *Hey, here's a possibility. Maybe I could become a California Closets consultant. I love closets and I love organizing. She probably doesn't make much money, though. Maybe I could own a franchise. Wouldn't have to go back to school to do this. They'd give me the training. Would this get boring though? Organizing people's closets day in and day out? And where would I get the money for a franchise?*

I mentioned in Chapter Four that I spent the day with an interior designer and did not enjoy it. So I crossed interior design off my list of careers to explore.

Image consultant. *What I really love are makeovers. I love those TV shows,* How Do I Look? *and* What Not to Wear. *I wonder what it'd be like to be an image consultant. I could definitely have my own business and probably could get started with very little training.* Conducted a few informational interviews with image consultants. Hired one to help me get my own wardrobe under control and then did an informational interview with her. *Did some research. There's no set career path here. Not sure most of them are making any money. Also sounds like hard work. Plus, am I really polished enough to be an image consultant? Do I really want to have to keep it together all the time?* That option's out.

Plus, all of this feels rather silly. I'm a lawyer. What are some more respectable career changes for lawyers?

Director of career services office (CSO) at a law school. *Now this could be a really good fit. I love talking to people about their careers, especially lawyers. And even though I don't like being an employee, it seems like there'd be some autonomy here and it's hard to knock a steady paycheck.* Did several informational interviews with folks in CSOs. *Feel a little wary because most CSOs are pretty traditional—focused on finding careers within the law for students, but some of them give you some leeway. After all, there's often a counselor who focuses on alternative careers for lawyers. I'd want to be something of a renegade here, though. Maybe there's a CSO that will let me take over and revolutionize it.* Went on an interview for a director position at a CSO. *Boy, I hope I get an offer. The salary feels low in comparison to working at a firm, but I played the What If? Game and it's doable. I'd be willing to trade dollars* *for career satisfaction.* Didn't get the job. *I'm so disappointed, but my dad told me I'd have been bored within a month. Wonder if that's true. They weren't really looking for a renegade. Plus, it's going to be hard getting my foot in the door at one of these jobs. The guy who interviewed me said some really nice things, but told me he felt it was safer to go with the person who already had some experience in a CSO. Read as, if they give me the job, I might be gone in six months. As much as that hurts, he could be right.*

Trainer/consultant. *Did this work in the past and don't love it, but maybe I could find some way to make it work.* Did an informational interview with a professor who does creativity consulting on the side. *Nice guy, but again, there's no clear path on this one. It's not like I teach this stuff at a university and have credibility to do this.* Read a book called *Drawing on the Right Side of the Brain* by Betty Edwards. *I love this book. Maybe I could become a trainer for the programs the author does.* Spoke to one of those trainers. *This is going to be a really hard field to get into. Not feeling too encouraged about this. I can't just keep doing the negotiation training, though. I need something of my own. Hey, maybe I could combine coaching with this!*

Coach. Did lots of informational interviews with coaches. Flirted with the possibility of hiring my own coach. *This is going to cost a lot of money— hiring my own coach, taking coaching classes (because I'm certainly not going into this without training). Not to mention—I hate to say this, but maybe I'm not suited to be an entrepreneur. It's hard being out here on your own—no social network like going into an office every day, Saturdays and Sundays feel like just another part of the week, no steady paycheck. I feel like I won't have much of an identity here.*

I don't know. Maybe I haven't given law a fair shot. I only practiced in one area and at one firm. What if I changed areas and tried a boutique?

Lawyer. Created a list of practice areas I'd like to explore—employee benefits, trusts and estates, and mergers and acquisitions. Did tons of informational interviews. *Employee benefits sounds pretty interesting. Like puzzle work. I have a good friend at a small firm who really likes the work and likes it there. She said she'd mention me to the name partners.* Interviewed at the firm and got an offer. *Forget changing careers. It's too hard and too scary. I'm going to* *see if I can make this work. Because if I can, that's the best possible outcome, isn't it? I'm using my law degree and earning a good salary.* Accepted the offer.

Note: I try to encourage my clients to treat the exploration of another legal practice the same way you treat the other career possibilities. Explore it—don't just leap into it the way I did. Truth here? I got scared. Very scared. If you end up doing what I did, the best thing to do is to get back on the roadmap, rather than spending your time berating yourself. It's a total waste of time.

For most of the first year at my new law firm job, I was pretty happy. I had a schedule, a social network, and a steady paycheck again. I learned something new. I liked the hours, the people, the structure of the firm. I had my status back.

Then the itch returned. *I don't like practicing law. I don't. I guess I could check out a few more areas.* Did some research on family law, transformational law, and mediation. *I don't like practicing law. I don't want to be a lawyer. Is there any way out of here? I feel so stuck. It's my own fault. I came back in.*

I have to admit, coaching still really appeals to me. Is that crazy?

Coach. Hired my own coach. *Working with her is fascinating. Partly because I'm changing and growing as a result. But also because I'm fascinated by the coaching process itself. I'd love to learn more. Maybe I could just attend an introductory session for a coach training program—it's free.* Attended the session. *The training courses sound absolutely incredible. But coaching as a profession? I don't know. Most of the people in this room are older than I am. Maybe you can only be a coach if you've had thirty years of work experience. Would anyone take me seriously as a life coach? Not to mention, do I really want to spend my day connected to a headset?* Continued working with my own coach and signed up for my first coach training class. Took the class. *I am so confused. This coaching stuff is pretty powerful. I love this class. What if I coached lawyers? That might be pretty cool.* Started toying with the idea of a business plan by reading books about how to write one.

But I don't like practicing law, so why would I want to coach a lawyer on how to balance life and law practice? Ick. Maybe I could be an executive coach. There's some prestige there. Plus, lots of companies are hiring those now. Then I could get a paycheck. I met some corporate folks in coaching class. No, I'm not interested in being a company's hired gun. *I don't give a crap about what's best for the company; I only care about what's best for the employee. What if I worked with lawyers like me who want to change careers? That would feel less hokey than being a life coach.* Took another coaching class, attended a couple of meetings of the local coach association, got to know some coaches. *I'm meeting people I really like. I finally feel like I fit somewhere! Could this be possible?*

Took a crack at creating a one-page business plan. Created a bullet point list of marketing approaches. *Am I actually thinking about starting my own business? Whoa, that's really exciting. And it scares the crap out of me. How will I make money? What will I live on while I try to make money? There's no way I can do this. Or is there??* Started saving money, became more aware of how I was spending what I had, cut back on the rewards I had to give myself for going into the law firm every day (fruit smoothies, massages, weekly splurges at the bookstore). *Maybe I can learn from the mistakes I made being on my own before. Maybe those aren't insurmountable. There are ways to deal with some of those issues—like building my own schedule, a social network, and saving enough money so the lack of a steady income isn't so stressful.*

That's enough for you to get a sense of how it works. Baby step by baby step, I was working my way through my roadmap, and the plan was evolving as I went.

That's how you work your roadmap—preferably minus the four-year detour to another legal job. See where your roadmap takes you. It's going to be an exhilarating journey.

QUICK TIP

Panicking at the idea that the road map won't lead you straight out of the law and into a career you love? Leaving the law isn't like becoming a lawyer. To become a lawyer, you took the LSAT, went to law school, and passed the bar. There isn't necessarily going to be that linear path to an alternative career. It's a bit uncomfortable, I know, but I promise you, it's also an exciting ride.

BE FLEXIBLE WHEN THE ROADMAP ISN'T WORKING

As valuable as I think the roadmap is, things don't always go according to plan. For example, it took me way too long to leave the practice of law. It wasn't for lack of trying. After a certain point, I knew what I wanted to do, but it felt unattainable. I felt as if I was never going to get out of that law firm.

Then one day my coach said, "Maybe where you are is where you need to be right now. What can you learn from where you are?"

My immediate internal reaction? "How dare she! I'm so miserable I can barely get out of bed in the morning. Must be nice to be in a position of doing work you love and calmly telling someone who's dying that where she is is where she needs to be." Luckily my coach was working with me over the telephone, because I wanted to throw her out the window.

I know this is a tough question, so before I tell you what I came up with, let me show you how I answered it in a different context first, one that may be easier to digest.

Recently I planned to put my car in the shop for repairs. It had a few bumps and bruises that I'd been meaning to take care of, but I had been putting it off. I finally gave myself a stern talking-to, filed the insurance claims, took the car to a shop to get the estimates, saved some money, arranged for a rental car, and scheduled an appointment. You see the hassle, right? This required a lot of planning.

The day the repairs were scheduled, I walked into the garage, patted my car on the bumper, and said, "Okay, you ready? The next time I see you, you'll be perfect." I got into my car, put the key in the ignition, and turned the key.

And nothing happened. I mean nothing. The dashboard was black. I tried again and all the lights on the dashboard began flashing.

My first instinct? To start sobbing. What in the world?! This can't be happening. I've spent a lot of time setting this up. I had to take care of a gazillion details before I could get to this point. And now you're telling me it's not going to happen?

I was enraged. I could feel the heat rising up the back of my neck and the beginnings of a migraine. Then out of nowhere, that question my coach asked me popped into my head—"Maybe where you are is where you need to be right now. What can you learn?"

Well, that made me laugh, took the heat out of the situation for the moment. After I took care of the details—calling roadside assistance and postponing my service appointment and rental car, I sat down to think about the question.

What can I learn? I can learn that no matter how much you plan, things don't always go your way. Even if you think you deserve it.

I can learn that those internal temper tantrums suck the energy out of me and have the tendency to take over the rest of my day.

I can learn to be grateful. It was steaming hot in Atlanta that day. At least my car decided it wouldn't start in the parking garage of my building, rather than breaking down on the interstate. I was able to wait for the tow truck in the air-conditioned comfort (and safety) of my condo.

The question took the wind out of my raged-filled sails. Mind you, it didn't change how I felt about the situation. I was entitled to be annoyed that this was happening. And there was something valuable to be learned from this situation.

Okay, now back to when my coach asked me the same question while I was at my law firm. It was too hard of a question to answer at the moment. I had to ponder it for a few days. Then I realized one of the things I could learn was compassion. Compassion for myself and for everyone else in this miserable situation. I knew then I wanted to coach lawyers, so what would be a better learning experience than getting stuck myself?

I could learn that just because you want something really badly and you say you're ready doesn't mean you'll get it right then. I think there was a lot of internal preparation going on before I left. I was building my courage, my strength, my bank account.

I'd spent several years nursing my dissatisfaction. This may sound crazy, but it's hard giving that up. Remember when you were little and you had a loose tooth? It's sore, it hurts, and you keep probing it with your tongue. You know it would be best to pull it out, but you're afraid. That's how leaving the law can feel. You know you'd be better off letting go of that pain, but it's scary. I could learn to let it go.

That simple (and yes, infuriating) question showed me there was at least a purpose, several purposes in fact, for me being at that firm right then. My answers didn't change how I felt about wanting to leave, but they did give me just enough patience to hang in there until it really was time for me to pull that tooth.

NOW LET ME CONTRADICT MYSELF—AGAIN

You know how I've been harping on making gradual changes, rather than jumping into the icy waters? Well, it doesn't always work that way. I do have some clients who do some exploration, come across an opportunity, apply for it, and they get the job. In a matter of weeks, they've launched their new career and are loving it.

It happens like that sometimes. I've been thinking about why that is. What I've noticed is that the people this happens to have come to me already having done a great deal of preparation. They know what success means to them and they're not afraid to shout it. They've already got a clear sense of how much enough money is and want to try to live a life based on that amount. They have some ideas about careers they want to explore, and their passion and conviction come across so loudly to a potential employer that they get snapped up just like that.

"What do they need you for, then?" you grumble. Good question. What I've also noticed about such folks is that when we work together, there's synchronicity. The opportunities appear, they grab them, and off they go. And I'm left wondering if I'm magic (probably not), if they could have done it without me (possibly), or if this relationship of client staying focused on her dreams and coach focusing on client's agenda only is powerful (which it is).

Could that be you? Possibly. I'm betting you know what you need— whether it's time to work your roadmap or no time at all because the opportunity of a lifetime just appeared in front of your face. Hint: If it's a legal job posting, it's probably not the opportunity of a lifetime.

INQUIRY: WHAT CAN YOU LEARN FROM WHERE YOU ARE RIGHT NOW?

Don't fight the question. If you can't answer it right away, give yourself a few days to think about it. Jot down your answers. You'll probably need to come back to them for strength later on.

HARD TRUTH

You should have seen this Hard Truth coming from a mile away. Maybe where you are is where you need to be right now.

CASE STUDY
• • • • • • • • • • • •

Jennifer Alvey, age 41
Writer, Editor, Trainer, Entrepreneur, WordSolutions.biz, Nashville, TN
9 years in journalism, less than 1 year in entrepreneurship
BA in Political Science/Transylvania University
JD/Duke University School of Law
Years of practice: 8

Type of practice: 1 year on the Federal Circuit, complex commercial litigation with focus on intellectual property, large and medium firms, Washington, D.C.

Jennifer has a roadmap that I bet she couldn't possibly have predicted. That may sound scary when you're used to certainty and structure, but I promise you it can also be an incredibly fulfilling journey. Notice all her career twists and turns, and pay special attention to what she discovers at each curve.

Will your roadmap look like mine or Jennifer's? Not necessarily. It could be a straight shot from your legal career to your alternative career. But if it's not, I think Jennifer would agree with me that what you gain along the way, in addition to insight about your career likes and dislikes as well as valuable work experience, is the courage to keep moving forward.

Describe what you do.

Currently I do freelance writing. I'm also starting [to offer] legal writing training courses [for law firm associates] because Nashville just doesn't actually seem to have much of that.

How did you get into your current career?

The last six or eight months I was at [the firm] I was just miserable...again. I said, "I have got to do something about this!" I finally found a career counselor that I really liked and enjoyed, and we just clicked together. And that was just helpful, enormously helpful to figure out that part of what attracted me to law in the first place was the writing and some of the reasoning. Other than that, I could just leave it in a second and it would never have bothered me.

I got my courage up and sent a résumé to BNA Books [a large legal publisher in D.C.] because they had an opening on one of their newsletters that does intellectual property. I came up with this beautifully crafted letter—a lot of angst went into crafting this letter. I was [going] out of town and I [asked] my housemate [to fax it for me], and I forgot to give her a résumé! So she dutifully faxed what I had given to her, and I get back [in] town and I had this email from the managing editor, who

[said], "Ms. Alvey, could you please send me a résumé?" And I [thought], "Oh no! I'm a moron!"

But it all worked out. What was really attractive to my manager was that I had a lot of intellectual property expertise. I knew what a patent application was, I knew what copyrights were, I knew what trademarks were, I had a vague idea what domains were. [BNA has] a writing and editing test that they give all the editorial applicants at BNA, and I did all right on that. So he hired me!

That was really amazing in retrospect. They are big on reporting at BNA and of course, I didn't major in journalism. We didn't even have any kind of communication classes in my undergrad. So I got on-the-job training for how to do reporting, which was fabulous. I learned a lot about the publishing industry just from being there and seeing what kind of products they liked to launch and just how a publication got put together. You know, all the sausage-making part of it.

I did that for a couple of years and then I was just exhausted from writing one or two stories every single day. It wears you down. I was just getting burned out, so I decided I wanted to try at least to do some freelancing and I had one sort of biggish client.

I found out [though, that] I was incompatible with [this client]. So I was looking around for other clients and then September 11 happened. I said, "Okay, I'm not going to freelance now, because I would like to eat!" And just being relatively inexperienced, I knew that at that point it just wasn't really the best move. When you have a gung ho, dot com boom market, it [is] one thing, but when everything was just really starting to pull in, I thought [it] was just not the time to be new at something.

[Deciding not to freelance] turned out to be a really good thing because I ended up finding a job with a trade magazine that was focused on the utility industry, of which I knew absolutely nothing. But, it was another thing that has just turned out to be a fabulous learning experience because I didn't know anything about magazines, I didn't know anything about utilities, and [learning about] particularly the magazine side of it was just wonderful.

I loved working on a publication that had images and layouts that were fun to look at because legal stuff is very much this sort of sea of gray. There is lots and lots of black print on white paper. It's not stuff that you read because it is so engaging; it's stuff you read because you have to. Working on a magazine and learning about how to entice people into the copy and make your stories really grab them up front, that was fabulous. I really enjoyed that.

And then I was actually on maternity leave when I got a call. I had seen a really intriguing ad, literally a year before. [The job] looked like it was the editorship of a legal magazine. It was a blind ad [and I applied]. So while I was on maternity leave, I got this call. [They said,] "I know it's been awhile, but would you like to come in and interview?" [I said,] "Okay, sure! Why not? I'm only sleep-deprived, but sure I'll come talk to you!"

[The job] turned out to be the editor in chief of the magazine for the Association of Corporate Counsel, which is called *The Docket*. And that was probably, in many ways, my most favorite job in publishing because you get to set the tone of the magazine, you get to talk to authors, you help take something that you know is a good article and help the author think about how best to put it together. And then it's got all of the visual elements, which are a lot of fun to me. And I just loved that job for so many reasons.

But then, it was in Washington and I had a kid who was going to turn 2 pretty soon, and [my husband and I thought,] "Okay, we have to find a house that has a yard bigger than the postage stamp of our townhouse." And we [were] looking around and anything like that was at least three-quarters of a million dollars. And I thought, I just do not want that. I do not want to be on the hook for that, because if one of us loses our job, it's going to be a catastrophe quickly. And you aren't going to have several months [to] look around. It's something that quickly is a problem. And just the commuting in D.C. was really starting to wear on my nerves fairly significantly. So we said, "Well, all right, let's look somewhere else."

We landed in Nashville because we wanted to be closer to family. My family is all in Kentucky. So Nashville just ended up being the place. You know, I have to say my tension level has certainly diminished quite a bit not having to deal with all of the grueling traffic and all of the "Type A" personalities all the time.

When I moved here, I had a job with a publishing company that [had] a human resources focus. They had me come on board to do their in-house counsel products. But then they abandoned that line of thought at the end of last summer and said, "Well, you know, we're not going to do that anymore, so we'll see you later!" So okay, fine with me! I was missing the variety of some of the things that I had done before. I was just kind of ready to be out on my own, and I felt like this time I had so much better of an idea of—I've been in the editor's chair, I know what editors need and want, and how to make them happy. I certainly didn't have that experience the first time around when I tried the whole freelancing thing. So [I started freelancing again. And] it is much better this time.

What fears did you have about not practicing law?

Well, it was such an unknown what a career path in publishing would even be. And I didn't even really think to myself, "Okay, I'm switching careers and I'm going into publishing now." It was never that conscious. People asked me, "Where does working at a place like BNA go?" They just couldn't see it. And I really didn't know the answer to that question either, but at that point I thought, "It has to go somewhere better than [where] I am now." That was all I really knew, was that it has to be better. And it was!

The pay was lousy compared to what you can make as an attorney. I was probably making less than half of what I had been making before, but [I was] doing something that I inherently enjoyed everyday. I quickly found out that that was a reward that I think so many attorneys do not really have in their work. They do it, and many of them do it well, but there isn't this inherent enjoyment of it. I do think that some lawyers have that, but most of the ones I ever worked with weren't those people for whatever reasons.

How do you define success?

Money is probably the last on that list. I mean, making enough to be able to pay your expenses and have the occasional extravagance is great for me. But I think it is doing something that you just really like, and that in some way, shape, or form, you would probably do anyway, even if you weren't paid. If you can do that and be a good human being on top of it, you know, be kind to children, pet dogs, whatever. If you can wake up in the morning and be glad about where you are, that to me is a success.

How did you know that this was the career for you?

When I didn't find myself hating the actual stuff that I did after six months or a year. I think it was just doing it and finding things about it that I enjoyed and looking forward to just learning more about what I was doing. And being excited when I did learn something new. It's like, oh wow, you can take this paragraph that was kind of a little boring and pull it out and make it a sidebar. And then it's great, all of a sudden your article gets better and you've got this nice visual element. I mean, that to me was just exciting. I think it was having those moments of, "Oh, this is cool" along the way that told me that this was basically the right area for me to be in.

What makes you different from lawyers who don't pursue their dreams?

I think I am, personality-wise, put together probably a lot differently than most people who go to law school. I have this very quirky, creative personality. It's not that there aren't quirky, creative personalities all throughout law, but what I saw was that many of those people really got sort of beat down. The ones who were the most miserable tended to get out, but the ones who were only somewhat miserable tended to stay in. For me, law was just never ever going to be satisfying.

In some ways, being as miserable as I was at times was a great thing, because it really made me find something different and really pursue that. So it didn't really feel like a blessing at the time, but in a lot of ways being as unhappy as I was was a great blessing. I guess the ability to look at it like that probably does make me different.

What pressures did you experience, if any, to continue practicing?

The only pressures I really felt were financial. That was really the only thing that ever made me even think about going back into law, but that just wasn't enough for me because that's just not how I am geared. There are plenty of people who, if they can amass a decent salary and the nice home in the very nice suburb and the 2.5 kids and whatever, they're pretty content with that. That [was] just never me. I just couldn't do it just for the money.

What doesn't appeal to you about practicing law?

Practicing law today is very, very difficult just because of the enormous pressure to be productive all of the time. Even when I was practicing, which was now almost nine or ten years ago, the billing pressure was pretty intense, and I think it has gotten nothing but worse in the last decade. I think that alone would scare me off wanting to practice, even if you like what you do, [even if] you're personality-wise put together for [practicing law], and you've got whatever other thing that it is that makes people happy [practicing law]. Being lawyers, I think just the pressure to bill just makes it a really unhappy place right now.

Also, collegiality really drops when you are under so much pressure, because you feel you do not have time. You know, the pressure to get results at any cost means that you may be taking some, if not ethical shortcuts, you're certainly not doing anything to build relationships. I think that when practice was more local (and this may be just the rose-colored glasses looking back five or ten years before I was actually practicing), I think there was more of a sense of, well, you can't really act so badly because it will come back to haunt you in your local community.

What is the purpose of work in your life?

Aside from the obvious one that we all have to earn a living, it's to do something that I feel has some meaning or will help somebody in some way with their lives. You know, when I was editing *The Docket*, I loved it because I knew that we did a lot of service journalism, a lot of how-to pieces, and I knew that that would help people in their jobs who were struggling with some issue. And if we could give them an article that would really help them out in a short amount of time, I loved that. I loved th[e] idea that we were able to do that for the people who got the magazine, just the idea that something that I do as part of my work is helpful to someone else.

Anything else?

I remember [the] desperation [of wanting to get out of the law] so vividly and I was so convinced that there was no such thing as a job that I would have fun at that I could afford to do. And I think we [put up] a lot of blinders because we are so scared. Just understanding that that is what you're doing to yourself a lot of the time is important. It's so much easier to see it in hindsight. But if you can't see it yourself, you need to find somebody who can help you see it.

And don't think that all of a sudden, once you hand in that resignation letter and you have this grand and glorious job, that it is all going to be a bed of roses. It might be a bed of roses, but they might have some pretty nasty thorns occasionally. It is work, after all. It is not all going to be perfect, but you know you're on the right track when you find yourself interested in what you're doing and not gritting your teeth and having to just really force yourself to do your job every day, which is, I think, how a lot of lawyers feel. That's just no way to go through life, it really isn't.

It's not easy because you're giving up the sort of "Good Housekeeping Seal of Approval" lifestyle in a lot of ways. If you've got a lot of people who think that you are just wasting your [legal] talents [by leaving the law]—you know, if all they've really been exposed to are these media images we have of lawyers as being these smart, successful people with lots of money—it's hard to turn your back on that. But you really have to listen to what makes you tick and what will put a smile on your face, and what will make you want to be kind to children that aren't your own. To make you happy that you got to know your kids a little better because you didn't have to work ten- and twelve-hour days, six days a week or seven days a week. It's not easy, but it's worth it.

• • • • • • • • • • • •

WHAT YOU SHOULD HAVE LEARNED IN THIS CHAPTER

☐ Your roadmap is also probably going to be one wild ride. It's going to make a great story, though, when you get where you're going.

☐ When working your roadmap, give yourself permission to be open, curious, and exploratory. This is not the time to be rigid, judgmental, or hostile.

☐ Rather than waiting for the magical moment when the career of your dreams knocks on your door, prepare for it so that if it does show up, you're ready to grab it!

chapter nine

Leaping Off a Cliff—Onto a Tall Stack of Fluffy Pillows

LETTER FROM A DESPERATE LAWYER

Dear Monica,

I've been all excited about leaving the law up until now. Now I'm just scared. Scared. I don't think I can do this. Help!

Clancy

At the beginning of the coaching relationship, my clients often say that leaving the law to pursue a new career feels as if they would be jumping off a cliff—with nothing to break their fall. It's no wonder lawyers stay at their legal careers. I'd take misery over breaking every bone in my body any day.

If I ever want my clients to make that free fall, my job as coach and their job as client is to build a gigantic stack of plump, fluffy pillows to cushion the impact of that leap.[22] Hang on a second and just think about that, because it's a comforting image that should make you smile. Stand at the edge of the cliff, look down and see a tall, tall stack of white, cushiony pillows, and then jump. Big difference huh? I want you to hold on to that image because that's what it's really about. I'm not suggesting that we can prepare for and cushion all blows, but we can certainly do better than you just deciding one day that you've had it and turning in your resignation letter that second.

Hopefully, you've realized that the chapters preceding this one are the pillows. But just in case you're still frightened—and don't worry, most of my clients are—let's hit the bedding store of your choice right now and stock up on more goose down.

MONEY

I had to come back to this topic. It's one of the biggest stumbling blocks for my clients. It's also one of the most important pillows. If you're taking a sabbatical, starting a business, or taking a lower-paying job, you have to get a grip on this issue. Even if you end up taking another job that pays you what you're making as an attorney, don't you want to know where your money is going and whether or not you want it to go there? It's worth it to experience the agony of discovering that your money is going down the drain in order to gain the clarity to make conscious decisions about how you want to spend your money.

If there's one message you take away from this book, please don't let it be that you should leap without thinking about money. Money serves a purpose. It pays bills and provides security. It buys groceries. But money is not the be-all, end-all. What I'm trying to get you to do is to find a way to loosen money's death grip on you. If you accumulate piles of it by spending your life doing something you hate, what have you gained? Don't discount this one. You can get so used to feeling miserable that you think this is what it's like to have a job. You tell yourself, "I'm supposed to have backaches, headaches, endless colds, etc. I'm supposed to feel like crap every day." No, you're not.

Or let's say you're making piles of money but what you earn is going out the door almost as soon as you make it. What choices are you making about how you spend your money? Most of my clients come to me saying that they can't make any significant changes in their lifestyles—every penny they make is accounted for. By the time we finish working together, their perspective on money changes. You've never seen such shifting of priorities to make room for the new lives they envision for themselves and their families. Sometimes it's easy and sometimes it's not. Sometimes it takes time and sometimes it doesn't.

ANGELS

You have to have angels. I'm not talking about the Biblical kind here, although those are nice to have, too. What I'm talking about are people who often come out of nowhere to support you in making your career transition. Unequivocally support you. Won't take no for an answer.

Let's talk about what these angels might look like, so you can learn to spot them and hold on tight.

Financial Angels

I described some of my money adventures in Chapter Seven. Let me add one more piece for you to think about here. A lot of lawyers I talk to have dreams of entrepreneurship. I was one of them. I've never liked being an employee. Someone telling you what to do, who to do it with, how to do it, and when to do it every day? Drove me nuts. I knew eventually I'd have to have my own company. Autonomy is a major value of mine. And over time I learned that the easiest way to satisfy that craving was to have my own business.

So how much money do you need to do that? There are a lot of books out there that will tell you. Let them guide you, but ultimately you have to make your own decision. After reading all the conventional wisdom, I settled on six months' worth of living expenses. (Yes, the amount I chose is nowhere near the amount suggested by conventional wisdom. Most authorities recommend one to two years' worth. However, I was convinced that conventional wisdom did not apply in my case. Once I opened my doors, lawyers would come pouring out of every office, courtroom, and government building in the land to beg me to help them find new and meaningful careers. More importantly, I was tired of waiting and figured six months' worth would have to do.) As a caveat, I should add that I did manage to stretch that six months of savings to cover nine months' living expenses. Still not enough, as it turns out, but I did my best.

I was smart enough to realize that perhaps it wouldn't hurt to have a backup plan. I'm not sure my parents know this, but I was planning on hitting them up for a loan. Not at that moment, but more of a backup loan for six months on an as-needed monthly basis.

Before springing this opportunity on them, I thought it would be wise to prepare my case with the assistance of my older brother, Walter. Walter is just as frugal as my father. So I figured Walter could come up with all the arguments my dad might use to stave off supporting his 30+-year-old daughter. As I anticipated, Walter came up with arguments I couldn't answer. I thought about it, crafted answers, and we polished them. After a few nights of this I was ready to contact the parental unit.

As I was wringing my hands the night before, going over my arguments in my head with an occasional question for Walter, I almost missed a comment that he made. What was the comment? He said, "I'll give you the loan." I was astonished.

Who could be your financial angel? Don't scoff and say, "Nobody." It could be a spouse, a parent, a relative, a business partner. Sometimes all you have to do is ask.

Inspirational Angels

These angels aren't necessarily the kind you'll spend a significant amount of time with. They may just be a blip in your day. Like the guy who waits on you at a restaurant and out of nowhere says, "You'd make a good teacher," (and that's the career you're thinking about pursuing). Maybe it's the brother of a friend you just met who says, "I can see why you'd want to pursue that career. I just met you and I can see you'd be really good at it." Perhaps it's a colleague who wishes you well in your new venture by saying, "I'm not surprised you're leaving. I could always tell you had bigger, grander visions. I don't have any doubt you'll succeed."

I find my inspiration everywhere. Have you seen the film *Strictly Ballroom*? It's an Australian independent comedy/drama about a competitive ballroom dancer who wants to dance his own steps when almost everyone around him believes in sticking to convention.

The ballroom dancer's lover spits out a Spanish proverb at him in disgust when he decides to give up his dream of dancing his own steps. The English translation of the proverb is: "A life lived in fear is a life half-lived." *A life lived in fear is a life half-lived.* Well, that scared the heck out of me. Isn't that what I was doing by continuing to stay at my firm?

I'm a rabid Agatha Christie fan. Yes, I even find inspiration in my beloved mystery novels. There is a passage in *4:50 From Paddington* that describes a young woman brilliant at math who is confidently expected to teach at the college level. She shocks everyone by becoming a domestic. She starts a business providing domestic services for wealthy, prestigious families. She does it all, but for tremendous sums of money and only for limited periods of time. After only a few years, this young woman, Lucy Eyelesbarrow, is known all over England and is a tremendous success. She enjoys her life tremendously and finds great satisfaction in her work.

After reading this passage, I decided that I wanted to be Lucy Eyelesbarrow when I grew up. No, not become a domestic, but turn people's expectations upside down and create an unconventional career for myself that would be a phenomenal success.

Keep your eye out for these angels. Not only note what they say, but create a space to keep those inspirations.

QUICK TIP

I actually created a document entitled "Inspiration." Anytime anyone or anything gave me a little thrill of inspiration, I noted it, who said it, and the date. When I needed a lift, I'd read this page from my angels. I still do, actually. I recommend you do the same.

Angels You Go Out and Get

Don't just wait for angels to come to you. Actively pursue some. If you can't afford a coach—and be careful before you make that decision because coaches charge wildly varying fees and if you can afford to splurge on that

Coach purse, then you can definitely afford a coach—remember that support group I told you about in Chapter Two. Go out there and put together your very own hand-selected group of angels.

Warning: Just as there are angels out there, there are also some folks just waiting to drag you down. Get adept at identifying who they are. And then avoid these naysayers, doom-and-gloomers, and doubters at all costs.

When I say get adept at identifying them, I mean trust your instincts. Some naysayers are obvious. They tell you the ten thousand reasons why what you want to do won't work. But there are others who are insidious. Like that friend who never actually says anything negative outright, but every time you leave her you're questioning your dreams, your hopes, your very existence. Or maybe they sugarcoat it and say it really sweetly, but the message is the same—forget about it. Those are naysayers.

It's unfortunate if you're close to your family members and one of them is in this category. You might want to read *Difficult Conversations: How to Discuss What Matters Most*[23] before trying to have a conversation with your family. There may be a way to help them get on your team. If not, you're going to have to keep your distance.

If it's a spouse or someone in close proximity to you—in other words, not talking to them is not an option—you have to protect your heart's desires. If someone is adamantly opposed, don't try to win him over. I tried that. It doesn't work. You're wasting precious energy and building doubts in your own mind every time you do. Accept that not everyone is going to agree with your choices, and spend your time with folks who do. Have conversations about what you want, what your dreams are, and what scares you with someone who is on your team.

RISK AVERSION PROOFING

It's the chicken or the egg dilemma—did law school attract you because you were already a risk averse person, or did law school make you a risk averse person? It doesn't matter. Either way, your fear of risk has a stranglehold on you. It's not a surprise. You can't study case after case of what can go really wrong when someone has a bright idea without it affecting you to the core.

My clients articulate so many fears. Fear of failure, fear of loss of status, fear of what others will say, fear of making a mistake. We've talked about ways to overcome these fears—articulate them clearly, reality test them. But I don't want to give you the impression that fear goes away. It doesn't. You can learn to manage it. But most importantly, what you eventually have to do is *feel the fear and do it anyway*.[24]

When fear threatens to cripple my participants, has them tiptoeing to the edge of the cliff to look over and shuddering, rather than making the leap, I challenge them to face the fear. Let's take a look at my conversation with Lindsay, a real estate lawyer who wants to find a job in sports management.

MP: Okay, let's play out the fear.

LINDSAY: What do you mean—pretend it really happens?

MP: Yes. You sound a bit frightened.

LINDSAY: Maybe.

MP: Feeling like if we talk about it, it will come true?

LINDSAY: Well, I know that's kind of silly. I also know I hint around this thing all the time, though.

MP: So I'm challenging you—let's play out this fear.

LINDSAY: Okay, I accept the challenge.

MP: So your biggest fear is failure. What's the worst-case scenario?

LINDSAY: The worst-case scenario. Okay. The worst-case scenario is that I try out this career, it doesn't work out, and I get fired. I won't be able to pay my bills. I'll lose my home. My family will be disgusted and walk out on me. My firm won't take me back. I'll end up living in a cardboard box on the streets. People will walk by, point me out to their kids and say, "See what happens when you try to leave the law?"

MP: Well, your laughter tells me how realistic you think that sounds.

LINDSAY: Yeah, that was pretty funny.

MP: Weight off the shoulders?

LINDSAY: Yes.

Worst-case scenarios are often phantoms. When I ask my clients to play out their fears, some of them can't even figure out how they would play out because they're so farfetched. Others can play them out and end up like the client in the previous example, laughing at how ridiculous they sound. For those rare times the worst-case scenarios are real, my question for my client is, can you live with that? Not that it will necessarily come true—it is, after all, the worst-case scenario. But if it did come true, could you live with it? Often the answer, and it surprises my clients, is, "Yes, I can. I could live with it and get over it. I'd rather try than continue being miserable."

My own worst-case scenario was that I'd have to go back to the practice of law. Guess what? My worst-case scenario came true. I came back to the law and practiced for four years before starting my coaching firm.

But it wasn't at all the horror I thought it would be. I envisioned I'd be forced to return to the law. But I wasn't. I actually decided I wanted to try law again. I wasn't sure whether I'd missed out on a legal career that would work for me.

I also envisioned that people would chastise me or, at the very least, make some sort of snide comment about how I'd failed to make it. In fact, when I interviewed at the firm, everyone thought what I did in the interim was interesting. It was as if they admired me for making the leap. So my worst-case scenario actually came true, and I lived to tell the tale.

SOMETIMES LEAVING THE LAW DOESN'T MEAN TOTALLY LEAVING THE LAW

If you start a new full-time job outside the law, that's leaving cold turkey. But sometimes you can cushion the transition by making a different kind of change.

- Maybe you want to have your own business, but want to build it up first.

- Maybe you want to pursue work that, for now, doesn't fully cover your living expenses.

- Maybe you want to find a way to practice law in some sane form or another, just not full-time.

I know I talk a lot about leaps and icy cold water and cliffs, but the truth is that sometimes leaving the law is a slide down a gentle slope. Some of my clients aren't ready yet to escape from the law altogether, but they are checking out bus schedules to see when the next bus will be barreling in front of them because they desperately want out of their current stressful, unfulfilling legal jobs. That still counts!

For example, one of my clients wants to open a bakery. But she's not ready to do that just yet. She wants to save money, train for her new career, do some preparation. So first she left her stress-filled, overwhelming law firm for a slower-paced, more collegial legal job. She's taking pastry classes and selling cakes to friends for their special occasions. Next she'll go to pastry school, do an externship. Then she'll open her own bakery.

A fellow coach practiced law at a large firm and then started her own practice. She discovered coaching and began to take classes. She continued practicing law while she completed her coaching classes and built her coaching business. After several years of fulfilling double duty, she gradually eased out of her legal practice to full-time coaching.

A friend did some firm-hopping until she landed at a firm she thinks is the place she needs to be for now. In her off-hours she completed a novel. While she's working to get her book published, she's also musing over several possibilities for her next step—from adapting her novel for film to representing musicians to getting a doctorate in creative writing.

REALIZING THE WATER IS WARM

You know those baby steps I keep harping on? For us all-or-nothing types, that kind of approach is infuriating. Individually, those baby steps don't seem like much. They didn't seem like much to me either—taking a few coaching classes, getting my first clients. But it's more than that—baby steps add up. Because what you're also going to experience is the empowering sensation of being engaged by this work and realizing that you're good at it. Don't just gloss over that last sentence; those are two major things that my clients crave in their lives, and I bet they're important to you, too.

It should be encouraging news that the place you're headed isn't that icy cold water with sharks you're envisioning. In fact, the water is warm, so you should jump on in with the rest of us recovering lawyers. That's one big pillow.

WHAT ELSE DO YOU NEED TO CUSHION YOUR LEAP?

I don't have all the answers. Take a minute and jot down what comes up. Mull over this question as you continue on your journey and add what needs to be added. Then go out and get it.

HARD TRUTH

Now just because I'm talking about building a tall stack of fluffy white pillows doesn't mean that this stage goes on forever. If you're waiting until you get your stack just right, you're going to be doing more waiting than leaping. How many pillows is enough, you ask? Ignore your Gremlin and trust your intuition on this one.

CASE STUDY
· · · · · · · · · · · ·

Erica Hashimoto, age 37
Assistant Professor, University of Georgia School of Law, Athens, Ga.
4 years in education
BA in Government/Harvard College
JD/Georgetown Law Center

Years of practice: 7

Type of practice: 2 years on the Federal District Court, 1 year on the D.C. Circuit, and 4 years at the Federal Public Defenders Office as an Assistant Federal Public Defender in Washington, D.C.

I talk to so many lawyers who think that they would like to teach at a law school. That's why I'm delighted to share this interview with Erica with you. What I love about Erica's story is her insistence upon not having regrets in life, not reaching an advanced age and looking back wishing she'd tried certain things. She speaks more eloquently about it than I can, so I'll share her thoughts on that.

What about you, though? What would it be like to give yourself permission to make the leap, even if it means making a mistake, so that you don't have regrets about not doing it later in life? Maybe it's time to make that "jump off a cliff," as Erica calls it.

Describe what you do.

I teach four classes per school year to law students, and I do academic writing on indigent defense primarily. I serve as an advisor to student organizations. I've also become more involved in some of the state lawyer organizations. I've done training and work with, for instance, the Georgia Public Defender Standards Council, the public defender for the State of Georgia, and I'm on the Chief Justice's Commission on Professionalism.

How did you get into teaching?

After about three years at the Federal Defender's Office, I realized that I was getting burned out. I watched a lot of my clients go to jail, and I had gotten to the point where I was just really sad about it. I definitely took my job very personally, I think, and I realized that it was not healthy for me to stay in that atmosphere because I had too many clients and I was just taking it all very personally.

Luckily, I had a very understanding boss, so I went to him and I said, "I don't know what I'm going to do, but I think I need to leave." So I quit my job there before I had another job and applied to several law firms.

A number of law firms were looking for people with federal court experience because most of their lawyers had never seen the inside of a courtroom, particularly firms that wanted to see themselves as being in white collar criminal defense cases.

So I had offers from a couple of firms, but couldn't really quite see myself going to a firm because part of the reason that I loved being a litigator so much was that I felt like I was always fighting for the underdog. I wasn't sure I'd feel that way if I was working for a law firm that was charging $300 dollars an hour.

The other thing I was thinking about doing was trying to hang out a shingle on my own. There were a couple of other lawyers in Washington, a couple of women who were practicing on their own, doing criminal defense, primarily court-appointed where you'd get reimbursed. My thinking was that I could control my caseload and not have as many cases, and that it might alleviate some of my feeling of being burned out.

I have a friend in D.C. who is a law professor, and he encouraged me to think about going on the market and being a law professor. My real difficulty was that I hadn't published anything, ever.

[Hiring law professors] is a very centralized hiring process. There is what is known as "the meat market" in Washington, D.C., at the end of October or the beginning of November. All of the law professor applicants and representatives from all of the law schools all meet in D.C., and the forms of all the applicants are distributed to all the law schools in advance.

They set up thirty-minute screening interviews based on all of those applications, and then call back to campus anybody that they are interested in. So basically, for the cost of registering for this conference, your form gets distributed to all of the law schools, and then, if it works, it works. If it doesn't, it's not like you've had to send résumés to every single school individually.

So, I asked the law firm to keep the job open for me until I went through this process. I said, "I'm just going to go through this process and see what happens, and if something doesn't work out then I'll come to the law firm." I told them that my thought was that I probably would end up at the law firm. Part of my thinking on that was that I needed some recuperation time. I [also] figured that it would be good for me to do something [such as practicing at a firm] that I didn't feel quite so personally strongly about. I felt like I probably wouldn't care quite so much that it might be a good break for me to be at a law firm.

So, [the firm] agreed to keep [the position] open, and I went through the D.C. interviewing process.

It was actually really interesting because I think most of the people on the market (a) had been at law firms, and (b) had thought a lot about becoming law professors. They were, in a lot of ways, much stronger than I was on paper; what they were weaker at was interviewing. Because I was a trial lawyer, I can answer any question in an interview because I am used to thinking on my feet much more. So I got a bunch of call-back interviews to come back to law schools.

Tell me about the callback interview process, too, because I would imagine that's something some of my readers would be interested in.

You go to the school and you meet the entire faculty. It's usually a day-long, or in some cases, a two-day-long process. You do small group interviews with everybody on the faculty and then you do usually about an hour-long presentation of either something you've written or a work in progress, or something you're thinking about writing.

The presentation format is usually about 20–25 minutes of presentation and then you take questions from the faculty for another 30–35 minutes. I did about nine callbacks at schools all over the country, and came to actually really like my topic. I was talking about defendants who represent themselves in criminal cases, who go pro se, and people were interested in the topic enough that I had nice conversations with faculty members about it. So then I came out with offers to go to law schools all over the country.

And you know, I really had to think about whether at that point if this made sense for me, whether this was the right move for me. And part of the difficulty for me was that I had no offers in any city where I knew a lot of people. So, no matter what, if I took a teaching job, I was going to be taking a leap of faith and moving to a place where I didn't really know people.

Ultimately, I loved Georgia when I came here and visited, and just about from day one—this is probably not the wisest job-seeking strategy—I told all of the schools that Georgia was my favorite, and if I got an offer from Georgia I was going to go to Georgia.

What I ultimately decided was that this [job] was the perfect blend for me because I can't see myself never trying a case again and never having a client again, but it's very difficult for me to imagine myself ever doing what I did at the public defenders office again. You know, having seventy clients who I am always responsible for, who are always hanging over my head and who I'm freaking out about. This [job] gave me the opportunity to do a few different things simultaneously. One was to affect students, and to get students out there doing work that I think is really important. The second was to write about what is actually going on, on the ground, and to have that be a part of the academic discourse. And then the third thing is, I knew I wouldn't try cases for a little while, but my schedule is flexible enough that I can eventually represent a client here or there. And I can do it without charging them because I have a full-time job.

To me, it seemed like the perfect solution.

What fears did you have about not practicing law?

I miss my clients very much. I loved a lot of my clients. Particularly if you are in the criminal defense field, you get to know your clients very well because they're going through, for most of them, what is the scariest thing that has ever happened to them. You are their source of support.

That is what burned me out about it, but at the same time, part of the reason it burned me out was because I liked them so much.

I miss being in trial because trials are the highest highs and the lowest lows—much more so than any other form of public speaking or anything like that because the stakes are so high. And if you actually get an acquittal for your client, and it's somebody you've gotten to know—you know their family, you know their grandmother, you know their kids—there is nothing quite like it.

It's also the hardest thing in the world when you hear the word "guilty" and you know your client is going to go to jail for a very long time.

The third thing is that I was very close to my colleagues in my old office, and we all felt like we were in it together, and so we were all very close in that way. People were pretty tough, but they always had my back and I knew that. It was a very collaborative environment.

Define success.

Career success for me generally—and this does not just apply to the job I'm in—but it's very important for me to feel like I'm making a difference. For instance, the prestige of the school at which I teach is less important to me than the effect I feel like I'm having on the community I'm in. I feel pretty strongly that if I'm not affecting anything or anyone, then I am not successful.

One of the other reasons that I left the Public Defenders Office was that I felt like I wasn't able to have a healthy personal life because I was so tired all the time and angry with the world. So, part of success is finding balance between personal life and career.

How did you know this was the career for you?

I didn't exactly. I can say I knew that there were certain things that were not for me. I knew if I went to a law firm, it would not have been for longer than two years because I just don't think my personality is cut out for a law firm.

What I felt was that there was enough of a chance that it was going to work out, that it was worth the risk of jumping off the cliff. And as I say, I didn't think that I had it in me to stay, doing the kind of practice that I had been doing.

So I was definitely feeling lost trying to figure out, if not this, then what? You know, because I had already had one of the best jobs ever in a lot of ways. So I guess I just felt like there were enough good things about this job.

I wasn't sure I'd be a good teacher, and that was the part that I was the most worried about. Actually, that's not true. I was more worried about whether I would be a good academic, because you know, the whole writing articles thing. It is just kind of jumping off a cliff and saying, "I'll work hard at it and do the best I can, and hopefully I'll be good at it and make it work," but I didn't have very much assurance.

When I look back on it, I'm surprised I actually took the leap. I think part of what helped me a lot was that the schools that I interviewed at— and particularly Georgia—were so convinced that I could do it. They felt like I could, and my recommenders thought I could, and I trusted their judgment.

Any kind of lightbulb moments or aha moments?

The academic side of it was always the side I wondered whether I'd be good at. I wrote an article about pro se defendants, felony defendants, and it got published in the *North Carolina Law Review*. There was just a case before the Supreme Court on pro se defendants, and Justice Breyer talked about my article in oral argument. *Fulton County's Daily Report* did a front-page article on me about that.

It has been nice because it's an area that I feel pretty strongly about— the right of defendants to represent themselves. Because of that [experience], I feel like I actually did have a measure of success in the area that I was most worried about, which is the academic writing.

What makes you different from lawyers who don't pursue their dreams?

My one philosophy in life, to the extent that I have a philosophy about life, is that I never want to look back on my life and say, "I wish I would have," and feel like it's too late. And I think all of the decisions that I have made along the way in my legal career, none of which have been particularly traditional, even my decisions about careers before I went to law school, have been pretty nontraditional. [Prior to law school, Erica worked for one year at Gang Peace in Boston doing gang mediation and alternatives for youth and gangs, and another year at Project Free, doing community organizing in public housing developments in Dorchester, Mass.]

Part of my thinking was always, "If I don't do this, will I, when I'm 65, 70 years old, say, 'Why didn't I do that?'" And I think that has gotten me through a lot of the hard decisions where I have taken the nontraditional route. That, and I've been really lucky, because I've had a lot of opportunities.

I would rather in a lot of ways make a bad decision, try something, and have it not work out, than to turn it down and to look back and say, "What would have happened if I would have actually tried that?"

What pressures did you experience, if any, to continue practicing law?

Primarily just the internal ones. It's always scarier to do something you don't know how to do than to stick with doing what you do know how to do.

What doesn't appeal to you about practicing law?

Part of the reason that I was worried about hanging out a shingle is I would just be a disaster at charging clients. [Practicing law] is a service profession, which means you've got to ask people to pay for your services. I'm just a disaster at that. That cuts out a lot of jobs for me as a lawyer.

What is the purpose of work in your life?

It's helpful to pay the bills, but also I get a lot of personal satisfaction out of working. It's important to me to get personal satisfaction out of it.

Anything else?

I think very different things work for very different people. So, there are certain people who can find happiness working at a law firm, for instance, and that's good for them, and they should be there if it makes them happy.

But, there are other people who just never will. And so for those people, and I count myself in that group, you've got to just figure out what it is that will make you happy.

It's not a judgment that law firms are bad, or that a particular type of practice is bad. It's just a matter of fit for different personalities and different styles.

I do think a lot of it has to do with how you define success, generally speaking, because for me, it is much more important that I feel on balance that I'm doing something to make the world a better place.

I know that sounds too idealistic to a lot of people, but that is what is important to me. And since that's what is important to me, I can't find that at a law firm. Once I know that, then it gives me a lot more focus, I guess.

I'm happy for people who have different goals than I do and who can find happiness in places where I can't. But I also know myself well enough to know that I'm not them, and to try to make myself be them would make me unhappy.

• • • • • • • • • • • •

WHAT YOU SHOULD HAVE LEARNED IN THIS CHAPTER

☐ This journey is not just about figuring out what you want do—it's also about building your muscle for making the leap.

☐ Keep your eyes and ears and heart open for angels because they are everywhere.

☐ Come on in, the water's warm!

chapter ten

What Are You Waiting For?!

LETTER FROM A DESPERATE LAWYER

Dear Monica,

There is indeed a life after the law, as we defined it in law school at Penn. We all decided to go to big firms and many of us are not very happy. Four years ago, I thought going in-house would help me turn the corner. Two years ago, I thought leaving the law entirely for a business role would be the fix. Well, finally, I decided to do what I've always wanted to do. I've started up my own solo practice, and more recently, a high-tech consultancy called VR Workplace in a unique and emerging (and fun) field. I've even taken improv classes and written a stand-up comedy routine that I'm planning on trying out soon. My practice and consultancy are slowly taking off and I'm confident that things will work out because I'm passionate about what I'm doing. This shift in approach is me, at 36, with two young children, realizing that life is just too short to spend working on things that don't make you happy personally and professionally. I wish I had done this sooner.

Dave Elchoness

Where are you at this point? Are you somewhere on the roadmap, feverishly plotting your path? If so, excellent! I look forward to you sending me an email to let me know what you're up to.

Or are you feeling run down? You've done quite a bit of work. It's not that you're being a slacker. It's just that the check marks on your list are piling up, and you're still not seeing a way out. This just feels really hard.

A FEW WORDS ON FEELING LIKE YOU'VE RUN OUT OF STEAM

Let me tell you a little story about Sara. Sara wholeheartedly plunged into the career transition process. We came up with a few exciting possibilities, she conducted informational interviews, took on some short-term projects, and gathered a lot of information—just like you have been doing if you've been completing the exercises in this book. She did all of it with an incredible amount of energy. She thought she might like to be an interior designer. Sara even created a plan for leaving her legal job—saving some money, having the talk with her spouse and parents, baby steps to move into the career. And then all of a sudden her energy petered out.

Here's our conversation:

SARA: I don't know. I just can't seem to figure this out. I have an idea of what I want to do and I've got a plan to do it, but things just aren't happening.

MP: What do you want to happen?

SARA: Well, shouldn't some doors open or something? I'm not expecting miracles, but it seems like someone should do something.

MP: Who?

SARA: I don't know—*someone*!

MP: You should get a telephone call or something. Or some opportunity should pop up.

SARA: Yeah.

MP: Ready for a hard truth?

SARA: Uh oh. Okay.

MP: Sounds like you're waiting for someone else to do something instead of doing something yourself. What do you think about that?

SARA: That's right. You're dead on. It's just that I feel like this is too hard.

MP: Like it's a grueling journey. Like the stories your parents told you when you were growing up, about how they used to walk eight miles to school. In a blizzard. Uphill.

SARA: Exactly!

Sara described the career transition process as tough. By doing so, she's making the choice that it's going to be hard. Now don't freak out on me and think I'm getting all metaphysical on you. I want to talk about something that's important to this process.

I ask Sara to imagine there's a huge circle on the floor and to divide the circle into eight pie slices. Each wedge represents a perspective, a way of seeing this career transition process.

I ask Sara to stand up because we're going to move around this circle. We're going to play the *"What's Another Perspective?" Game.*[25] Together Sara and I are going to come up with a few more perspectives on how she might see making a career transition. As we name a new perspective, Sara will step into another wedge and that wedge will become that perspective. I'll ask Sara to describe that perspective, experience it while she's in the wedge, and then we'll move on.

We've already got one perspective. It's the one Sara described, the hard way. Let's label it "Uphill Journey."

MP: Okay, so "Uphill Journey" is one perspective. Step into another wedge. What's another perspective?

SARA: You mean, how else might I see making a career transition?

MP: Yeah. Don't think too hard. Actually, just blurt out whatever comes to mind.

SARA: Uh, okay. Rollercoaster.

MP: Good. Rollercoaster. Describe a rollercoaster for me.

SARA: It's like a topsy-turvy adventure. You fasten your seatbelt and as the rollercoaster starts chugging, you feel it in your stomach. It's excitement, it's fear. But it's a good kind of fear because you know you're safe, right. You're on a course. And it's going to be a wonderful ride.

MP: Okay, you feel that?

SARA: I feel that.

MP: Good, then, we'll call that perspective "Rollercoaster." Step into another wedge. What's another perspective?

SARA: Um...

MP: It doesn't have to be something concrete. It could be a color, an image, a fruit even. We'll work with whatever comes to mind for you.

SARA: Okay, blackberries.

MP: Blackberries. What comes to mind?

SARA: Well, they're tart and sweet. Substantial yet light. Summer fruit. Light and easy.

MP: Light and easy, huh?

SARA: Yeah, maybe this could be light and easy. Like summertime. Meeting new people, going new places, exploring new things, it's all easy.

MP: What's this perspective called then?

SARA: Let's call it "Summertime."

MP: Good. You feeling it?

SARA: Yeah, that's weird. I actually do.

MP: Great. Step into another wedge. What's another perspective?

SARA: I don't know.

MP: What about a thunderstorm?

SARA: That makes me think of that story of Benjamin Franklin outside in a thunderstorm with a kite.

MP: Okay, what about it?

SARA: Trying possibility after possibility for the sheer joy of it. It's a game. The more mistakes you make, the closer you are to a solution.

MP: What do we call this one?

SARA: "Thunderstorm" works.

We create eight perspectives total. Then Sara gets to choose which perspective she wants to have about making a career transition. She can choose "Uphill Journey," where she started, or one of the other ones we came up with.

Think of three or four people you know, very different people. I'll bet each of them approaches life in a different way. They all have different perspectives. If something happens to them, they look at it and respond to it in different ways. For example, I have a friend who I would classify as the eternal optimist. She's not a Pollyanna by the way. She has hardships, just like the rest of us, and gets scared and overwhelmed. But she somehow manages to see the good in everything, in spite of that.

I wouldn't classify myself as a pessimist, but I would say I'm a realist. I can see what's possibly going to go wrong in every situation.

Which one of us is right? That's not the point. The point is that my friend and I, and you and the people you thought of, have different perspectives and we view our lives through our variously colored lenses.

What's exciting about that is that it means you get to choose your perspective. You can choose the one you always have or you can choose something different.

Sara's skeptical (probably like you) but she plays along. She chooses "Rollercoaster," so I ask her to step into that perspective, literally. I have her find the wedge on the floor that's labeled "Rollercoaster" and step into it. Now that she's chosen a perspective, we're going to make a list.

MP: Okay, from this perspective of "Rollercoaster," from the perspective that making a career transition is going to be a wild, safe, enjoyable ride, what do you want to do next? Let's make a list of three to five things. We're just brainstorming right now, so don't feel locked into the list. You'll get to choose what you want to do from it. But remember it's from this perspective.

Sara: From this perspective?

MP: That's right. You're standing in it. Get yourself feeling it again. And once you're there, tell me what you want to do.

Sara: Okay, I'm feeling it. From the "Rollercoaster" perspective, I want to sign up for an interior designer program, take an entrepreneurship class, or talk to some of the design firms I met to see if I can get a job with them to build experience before I start my own thing.

MP: Feels like a rollercoaster, huh?

Sara: Absolutely.

MP: Good. Anything else?

Sara: Heck, you can be an interior decorator (rather than an interior designer) without a license, so I could hang up my shingle now and do it on the side. That's an easy gig to start while I'm still practicing. Or here's another one. I could apprentice myself to someone, even. There's a woman I met that I really liked who said I could work with her if I'm willing to do it for free. She has projects we could work on in the evenings and on weekends.

Great. We have a list from the "Rollercoaster" perspective. Now Sara gets to choose which activity she wants to pursue.

MP: Which one?

SARA: The last one. I'm going to call that interior designer and ask if I can be her apprentice.

MP: Great. When are you going to do that?

SARA: As soon as we get off the phone!

QUICK TIP

The fastest way to get new perspectives? Ask those three or four people you know who approach life in a different way than you do what perspective they would have about making a career change. Pick the perspective that appeals to you and adopt it as your own.

GIVE YOURSELF PERMISSION TO EXPLORE

Stop waiting for someone or something to give you permission to take charge of your career and life. I'll admit that I waited, too. I waited for someone to come to me, put a hand on my shoulder, and say, "Monica, I can see how unhappy you are. It's okay if you want to leave the law. You know what, it's more than okay. Go for it!" It's not to say that people weren't supportive, because they were. But nothing they said was enough. That's when I realized the permission I wanted had to come from me.

You deserve to have the work and life that you want. Don't just gloss over that line. Here it is again: *You deserve to have the work and life that you want.*

Just think back to what brought you here. What brought you to the point of buying this book, of hoping there would be something, *anything* in here that would help you magically transform your life? I don't know about the magic part, but I know that what this book contains has helped me, my clients, and the lawyers I interviewed leave the law to pursue fulfilling work. But it doesn't work by osmosis, as much as we'd like it to do so—you've got to take action, capture the learning, experience the growth for yourself.

What brought you here? Are you feeling restless, dissatisfied, unsure whether the law is your calling? Are the feelings stronger than that? Do you absolutely dread Monday mornings, and Tuesdays, and Wednesdays…are Sundays hard days? Are you having trouble getting out of bed in the morning? Does it take everything in you not to freak out in the middle of the day when you're sitting in yet another pointless meeting? Do you cringe every time a partner sticks her head in your door?

This is not the life you were meant to lead. You know that. You have so much talent, so much passion, so many gifts to offer the world. Isn't it time you gave yourself permission to explore how you might make a contribution to society, a contribution that has meaning to you and a real impact on society?

This section isn't about leaving the law just yet. It's just about taking the first step. The first step is giving yourself permission to explore. Permission simply to explore, what if? To explore the possibilities.

Remember I talked about baby steps earlier? As much as you daydream about turning in that resignation letter, that's a big, scary step. Exploring what work might bring you joy, fulfillment—that's a baby step. Can you commit to that?

GIVE YOURSELF PERMISSION TO SCREW UP

Are you waiting until you can make this transition perfectly, seamlessly, smoothly? You're going to be waiting a long time. There is no such thing. Get out of your head and the world of dreams where you find the perfect career with the perfect salary and the perfect colleagues, where family, friends, and former colleagues throw you a ticker tape parade to celebrate, where all your office stuff fits into one neat little box, and where you experience no guilt, doubt, fear, or regrets. Forget it. It's not going to happen.

There is no perfect plan for leaving the law. There is no paint-by-numbers approach that works. Sorry. This book *does* contain a roadmap, a loose guide that you can use. But it's a meandering one, with lots of twists and turns. Some stuff will be helpful to you, some won't. That's okay—you're not hurting my feelings. As I tell my clients, "This is about *your* agenda, not mine. If I offer something you don't want, you can always say no or make a counteroffer." The same offer is open to you. I just want you to have lots of ideas, inspirations, and laughter to choose from so that you can cobble together your own path.

And if this is where you're waiting for me to promise that once you leave and start your new career, life will instantly be rosy, you can forget that, too. The transition can be tough. When I left the law to start my business, I had this vision of waking up early, stretching luxuriously, and padding on bare feet to my sunlit office to welcome the day with calls with ideal clients, words tripping off my fingers, and checks galore.

Once the honeymoon was over, I woke up bleary-eyed after spending the night worrying about how long my savings would last, tripping past objects in my overly furnished office that also served as a second bedroom, willing the ominously silent telephone to ring, and staring at a blank computer screen praying that some inspirational words would come.

I wondered almost every day whether I'd made a mistake. I was almost paralyzed with fear.

I called my coach, who said, "You're like a bird that has just been released from a cage. You don't know where to go." When you've spent years complaining and griping about how unhappy you are and then all of a sudden someone opens the door to the prison and you're blinking in the sunlight, you begin to convince yourself that the world is a big, scary, open place, and perhaps that damp, dank prison cell is mighty fine after all.

"What's the point, then?" you shriek. "What's the point of leaving something that makes me unhappy for all that uncertainty?"

THE POINT

Let me be clear. The uncertainty doesn't go away. But over time it does become less of a mantra to your brain. And you start to experience moments of inexplicable joy, a strong, growing sense of conviction that you've made the right choice, clear and multiple indications that you are having an impact on the world, days of being caught up in your work (and even on the days you're not, you know the feeling will come back).

GIVE YOURSELF PERMISSION TO CHANGE YOUR MIND

So maybe you leave to try something else and it doesn't work out. You don't like it, the money's not good enough, they let you go, or whatever. For whatever reason, it just doesn't work out.

Lawyers never want to hear about things not working out or you changing your mind—it is simply not done. It's not in the equation.

You have to allow it to be in the equation. Why? Because otherwise you won't allow yourself to make the leap without having all the answers. And guess what? You're never going to have all the answers.

The first time I left the practice of law, I decided I wanted out and took the leap almost in the same breath.

Granted, I had some opportunities at the time. I'd just been appointed a lecturer on law at Harvard Law to teach a negotiation class for a semester and a few friends promised to consider me for corporate negotiation training gigs they got. I had about three months' worth of savings and was living with my older brother rent-free.

But it was still very much a leap without all my usual anal-retentive planning. Once I realized how unhappy I was practicing law my first year, I felt like I had to get out right away. Never mind that I had doubts about whether full-time corporate training would be fulfilling. I convinced myself that it would be glamorous to live a life of unpacking suitcases in hotels, working with Fortune 100 companies.

Instead, I was bored. Fortune 100 companies turned out not to be that interesting. And I was lonely. Most of my trainer colleagues lived in other states. Turns out I hated unpacking suitcases in hotels. And I discovered that there was a crucial component of my career identity that was missing. I craved autonomy. Cookie-cutter training programs weren't doing it. Nor was working for someone else, even as an independent contractor.

Then, as I shared before, I got scared. I let my doubts take over. And I went back to practicing law. At first it was okay. I could do the work, I was learning, I liked my firm. And then it was definitely not okay. Once the honeymoon was over, I realized I definitely did not want to be a practicing lawyer; there was no practice group on earth that was going to meet my needs.

Here's the thing—I wouldn't call these mistakes. I needed to go through them. I'm not trying to pretty it up and tell you to call these changes *opportunities* or whatever euphemism you have in your head. I'm just saying I had to give myself permission to go through some changes to get to this point. You have to do the same.

GIVE YOURSELF PERMISSION TO CHANGE CAREERS

My clients spend a lot of time bemoaning the fact that they became lawyers—that they took the stupid LSATs, went to freakin' law school, took the bleepin' bar....If only someone had knocked them upside the head when they'd first considered the idea of law school, maybe they wouldn't have wasted their entire lives.

Help me understand how this helps. I've always found kicking myself in the butt to be a less than productive use of my time. Not to mention, it has a strange effect on my clients. Instead of motivating them to leave the law, this "mistake they made" requires them to do penance by suffering for the rest of their lives in the practice of law.

First of all, who said it was a mistake? Perhaps you were meant to practice law. Perhaps you've acquired skills and capabilities that will now allow you to do something else. Perhaps you made friends you wouldn't have otherwise met. Perhaps you've cleared the decks of a career that you thought might appeal to you. Well, now that's one thing you know for sure you don't want to do. Stop right here and answer this question: what have I learned from making this career choice?

Second, why do you have to do penance? Why, when you make a mistake, must you wallow in your suffering for years to come? "Well, because I spent all that money and put in so much effort to get here that..."

Let me get this straight. Because you spent $100,000+ and over three years of sweat equity, you now must live the rest of your life in a hellish existence? That excuse just isn't doing anything for me, and it shouldn't be doing anything for you either.

GIVE YOURSELF PERMISSION TO DO WORK YOU LOVE

Lawyers are masters of *what ifs*. I know your Gremlin is ranting and raving, "You can't do this. You've spent of this money and time to become a lawyer. What will your family and friends think? You're wasting your legal career. What if changing careers is a big, fat mistake?" It's a runaway train.

I've got your what ifs right here. What if changing careers is the most wonderful, glorious thing that ever happens to you? What if you pursue work that makes you eagerly anticipate each weekday? What if the Sunday afternoon blues are a thing of the past? What if you're happy, fulfilled, at peace, and having an impact on the world? What if??

HARD TRUTH

If you're waiting for permission from everyone else in your life—your spouse, family, friends, colleagues, boss—you may be waiting a while. I've had some clients do this the hard way. And the permission they got didn't end up coming the way they expected. It came via hitting rock bottom, a life-threatening illness, the last words of a dying loved one, or the proverbial pink slip. Don't wait for that. Do whatever it takes to make this happen. Give yourself permission.

CASE STUDY
• • • • • • • • • • • •

Chuck Adams, age 64
Executive Editor, Algonquin Books, Chapel Hill, N.C.
39 years in publishing
BA in English/Duke University

LLB/Duke University School of Law
Years of practice: 1½ years
Type of practice: Trust law at legal department of a bank in New York City

For those folks who had doubts about practicing even before they graduated from law school, Chuck is a kindred spirit. What distinguishes him, though, from the masses who put on blinders and accepted their fate and legal jobs is that Chuck made the most of his opportunities. Moved to New York City for a dull legal job? At least now you know New York City is where you want to be. Took the legal job because you thought you'd only be doing it a short time before going off to war but now you've discovered you didn't pass the physical? See that as an opportunity to take advantage of the time you would have been in the military to find a career you love.

Chuck's story shows what an incredible career you can end up having, even if all you've got to start is an instinct about what you might want to do, an adventurous spirit, an inkling of your talents, and the courage to be guided by your own definition of success.

Describe what you do.

I work as an editor now. I get submissions primarily from agents who have either worked with me and know me, know my tastes, know what I'm good at, and know what my company does, or from agents who have read about me or know my reputation. The function agents have is to keep me from having to read things that aren't right for me or the company. They're right most of the time, even though I don't buy most of what they send me.

I read a lot. In fact, I read constantly. I get about fifteen manuscripts a week. And I only edit or publish five or six books per year. I have the complete right to say no. I do not have the complete right to say yes. If I like something, I take it to the publisher and try to talk her into letting me pursue it. I've worked in this business long enough to have enough standing so that I'm generally given my way.

As an editor I spend a lot of time working with the author in getting it to be the best book it can be—[sometimes by] going in and actually doing some writing to smooth things out or correct mistakes, but more commonly by asking a lot of questions—"I see what you're saying here, but it doesn't make sense to me. How does this connect to things you've said before?"

I edit a mix of fiction and nonfiction. In this business and especially in the big companies in New York—I spent fifteen years at Simon & Schuster before coming to Algonquin and twelve years before that at what's now a division of Random House, Dell/Delacorte—you get pigeonholed. I was known as a very commercial editor and an editor who also worked well with celebrities. So I have done an awful lot of books with celebrities and I've worked on an awful lot of very commercial, best-selling books because I have an ability to work with very big egos and not get stressed.

What fears did you have about not practicing law?

They were more personal than anything else. My father had really, really wanted to be a lawyer himself. He was a child of the Depression and was not able to go to college. He had one year of schooling beyond high school. And he really wanted me to be a lawyer. He wanted me to go into politics. He was a politician in Virginia, a behind-the-scenes politician, liked to pull strings. I talked with him about my decision. He was very nice about it. I said, "It's my life and I have to live it." He was disappointed. That was probably my biggest fear, disappointing him.

I worried also that if I decided later I wanted to go back [to practicing law] it might not be easy, but I also doubted very seriously that I would want to go back and I was right.

How do you define success?

For me, it was happiness. I guess again because my parents were very poor for so much of their lives. Money meant a lot to them. And they were very, very focused on security and making the most money you possibly could. By the time I came along, they were never wealthy but they were comfortable, so I never wanted. I grew up taking for granted a lot of what I had.

So when I started thinking about what I liked and didn't like with law, the thing that bothered me most was I wasn't enjoying it. If I'm going to be doing a job, let's say at least eight hours a day or more than that, I should get some pleasure from it. And I wasn't enjoying what I was doing at the bank.

How did you end up in publishing?

I worked for the legal department of a bank, the trust division. Pretty dry. Deadly dry. Secure, paid well, boring as could be. I had started to have severe doubts about being a lawyer before I even graduated [from law school]. I took this job primarily to get to New York to find out what I did want to do. I figured that would be a great place to explore.

This was during the Vietnam War. I assumed I was going to go into the Service. I was going into the Navy Officer Candidate School (OCS), and it was a four-year commitment. I figured it would keep me out of harm's way, which is what I wanted. But then I didn't pass the physical because of a hereditary skin disorder that surprised me and thrilled my parents. All of a sudden I was handed back what felt like was four years of my life. Once I got to New York—because I really thought I'd be in the [bank] job six months to a year and then I'd be in the Service—once I got in the job I realized I wasn't happy. That's when I decided I would take the four years handed back to me and start all over again. Also, I was fortunate because my father had paid for my education. I did not have a stack of debt. So I was kind of free and clear to do what I wanted to do. And I felt very fortunate and I took advantage of it and never regretted it. Okay, I did [regret it] for a while because I was making lousy money when I started in publishing. [Laughter.] The job at the bank was decently paying and the job in publishing was nothing, $100/week. (My rent was under $100 a month also. That was even cheap for that time. I got a deal.) It was a shock for a while and I did think, "What have I done to myself?" I didn't have enough money to live on. But I managed to live through that and come out the other side.

When I realized I wasn't happy with what I was doing [at the bank] and that I was going to make a change, I found a headhunter. I went to see a guy there. I said, "Here's my résumé. I'll take the law degree off if it's going to be a problem. I want to get into communications, whether it's publishing, broadcasting, or advertising, whatever. This is what I want to do. I want to try that."

The first job he sent me for was at *Good Housekeeping* magazine to police the Good *Housekeeping* Seal. And I thought, "Well, no, that doesn't sound like fun to me." Traveling around the country making sure everybody was living up to their standards. I thought, "No, that's not right."

The next job I was offered was as a traveler, which is a sales rep, for Holt, Rinehart and Winston, which was then primarily publishing school and college texts. And I didn't want to do that. I didn't want to sell textbooks, but while I was at that interview the guy said, "Well, there's a job I've been trying to fill here and everybody I send them they reject, so I'm going to send you, too. I don't know what they're looking for. Maybe you can figure it out." So I went and they hired me.

It was a weird job where they wanted somebody who they thought was smart, who they could teach about publishing, who could sit there and watch the procedures, watch the way everything was done, learn how to do it and actually do some of it too, be functioning, but say, "Well, why is it done this way?" There's so much tradition here. They thought some of it was archaic and they could produce books in a more uniform way, like light bulbs with different watts. They wanted more uniformity. So they hired me to sit there and try to tell them what they were doing wrong. I came away thinking, "I think it's great the way it is. I wouldn't change a thing." But I learned the business. I spent five years with that company and then went on from there.

Having a law degree helped there. Within a year I was head of a department—I was on the production side—of four or five people. Then I got put in the fast-track management program. [The company] was owned by CBS at the time. I spent a year at CBS getting to know CBS. At the end of the year I'd been in the personnel department recruiting college students and MBAs for jobs there. At the end of the year when I said, "That's fine. I know the company. Where do I go now?" they said, "Don't you want to stay in personnel?" and I said, "No."

That's when I left CBS and went back into publishing, and that's when I made the move into editorial as a Managing Editor, which is a job that requires that you know both production and editorial. I did not know editorial, and so I shouldn't have been hired, but they were desperate and I think again the law degree impressed them. So they hired me and I learned the job.

A law degree intimidates people. The first thing they say is, "Well, we can't afford you." And I'll say, "I'm much cheaper than you think." If it's a job I want I don't care about the money. To make this kind of change that's something you have to accept.

I was young. There were no responsibilities. I did it at the right time. I think if I'd waited until I was in my thirties, I wouldn't have done it. I'd have become too settled by that point.

How did you know editing was the career for you?

I didn't when I started. I just thought "I'll take this job and see if it works." Once I was inside the publishing company I knew that I wanted to move to editorial because for one thing, I had always been an avid reader. And in college I had also done some editing. I always got really good grades at school for the most part because I could write—and really just express things better than a lot of people could. So I knew that I had a gift for it. Mind you, being able to write and being a successful writer are two different things because I don't have a thing in the world I need to say. There's not a book in me that's dying to come out. So I've been able to use my talent as a writer as an editor. Once I got started in publishing, I knew that I'd like to be an editor.

And also in college I was a rarity on my freshman hall. This was, remember, way before computers. I could type. In high school in lieu of a study hall I had taken a typing class. So the guys on the hall would give me their papers to type and I'd charge them twenty-five cents a page and type their papers for them. And most of them were really crappy writers. So I started rewriting their papers for them. I mean, I would see sentences that made no sense, so I would try to make sense of them. And they started getting better grades. And I started charging more. I had a little mini-industry going there for a while.

So I knew that I had a knack for that kind of thing.

What makes you different from lawyers who don't pursue their dreams?

I can't say without asking them directly how they feel about their lives but I am very happy with the way my career has worked out. I've been successful. I've had a great career. I'm not the most famous editor in the world. I'm not the most highly paid editor in the world. The truth is I made the decision quite a long time ago not to pursue any kind of administrative work in this business simply because I don't want to deal with the finances of it. I'd rather work with the authors; I'd rather work with the books. I've had opportunities to become Editor-in-Chief or Publisher at places and I just didn't want them. Because, again, I came into this business not to make money, not to get rich, although it would be nice, but to find satisfaction and to be happy. I don't want to give that up, so I've kind of clung to that.

I think if someone has pursued the law and is really, really happy with what they've done, feel like they've had a happy life career-wise, then there's no difference. We've done the same thing. But [there is a difference] if they look back on their lives and say, "God I've wasted my time. I've got a comfortable home and a great family. That part of my life is really happy." But if you don't look forward to getting to the office, if you can't wait to get home, there's something wrong.

But again, I grew up in the sixties. The focus was a little different than in the eighties. People started becoming more acquisitive. Our thinking was more in the line of peace and happiness.

What pressures did you experience to go the traditional route?

From my father, there were pressures to go the traditional route. He insisted I go to law school. That was not an option for me. I could have not gone to graduate school, but the war was going on and I wanted the deferment. He insisted it was law school or nothing, so I went to law school. I felt pressure to not disappoint him.

I felt some pressure from the Duke University School of Law administration to go the traditional route. Once they realized I was not going to
conform, the pressure was off but there was some initially. And also once
they realized I wasn't taking it seriously enough to be a great lawyer.

I didn't make many friends in law school. For one thing, most of them
were married. Another thing was that I worked as a House Master on
the campus to help my father out a little bit financially. I was able to get
room and a little bit of board, some money toward food by doing that.
So I lived with freshmen my three years of law school. Most of the
House Masters were law students, and the ones I really developed
friendships with were the ones who did the same thing I did. So I had
never felt part of the community. But I would like to know if those guys
turned out happy. I just don't know. They took it so seriously and
wanted it very badly. I remember winning a moot court debate against
somebody who was convinced he was going to win—because everybody
knew I wasn't serious. And I won the thing and he was just really
appalled that he'd lost to me because he was a much better student than
I was. And I didn't take that seriously when I won either.

*What doesn't appeal to you about practicing law? You mentioned it a little bit
previously—that practicing at the bank was dry, boring.*

Those are the parts that bothered me—the direction I was going in the
corporate world. Especially in the banking world. But there are many,
many branches of law that are much more interesting. What you can't
get away from, though, and this is part of what attracted me and part of
what appalled me about law, is that you're dealing with other people's
misery all the time. I guess the idea of that was also a factor in
convincing me that this was not something that was right for me. I felt
I was wrong for the law.

I worried that I couldn't separate myself from the people that I'd be
dealing with. The idea of occasionally knowing that somebody might be
right but there's a legal way to get around it to keep them from what
they might have deserved because of a technicality bothered the hell out
of me. And I wasn't sure I could be an effective lawyer in a situation like

that. You can't half represent your clients; you've got to go whole hog. There were a lot of things that bothered me about the law. But there are a lot of professions that might bother me, like tax collector. [Laughter.]

What's the purpose of work in your life?

Obviously to put food on the table, but for me it's been a major—oh God, I can't imagine my life without this. It's defined me in many ways. I'm an editor. I'm recognized as an editor. I'm proud of what I do. I've gotten to work with amazing people. I've had incredible happiness. And disappointments, of course, but incredible happiness from seeing people and books succeed that I cared a lot about. I take it home with me every day. If I don't take the actual work with me, I know it's never out of my mind. It's why here, approaching [age] 65, I have absolutely no intention of retiring. Fortunately, I work with a company that doesn't really want me to. They want me to keep going, as long as I'm willing. It's something I want to keep doing.

Part of it is the experience of being an editor. I describe it as "falling in love." I always want to find the next book that's going to make me excited, that's going to change the world, if you will. And every time I open an envelope or open up a box that comes from an agent I am ready to fall in love right there. It's like when I was young and I would go [out] and think, "I'm gonna meet somebody. I'm ready to fall in love tonight." Rarely, rarely, rarely does it happen, but when it does it's incredibly exciting. I just don't wanna give that up.

I think also that even after I do retire from an office job I can continue to edit because I can do it on a freelance basis. A lot of people use editors to prepare the manuscript before they even get to the publisher. And I believe I could make extra income doing that. I will probably end up doing that some day, if my brain and everything else holds up.

Anything else?

The motive for me was always that if I didn't think I was going to be happy with what I was doing, I wouldn't be any good at it. I figure there are enough crappy lawyers out there without me becoming yet another one, one who says, "I'm making a decent living, doing my job, but not really invested in it." It comes out of the reason I thought I wanted to go into law. I wanted to be a good lawyer. I wanted to do good work. And I felt at best I was going to be a mediocre lawyer.

I'm a helluva good editor. And I take great pride in what I do. And I take pride in the fact that I've succeeded. It's a very tall pyramid and I climbed my way up. And that's gratifying. That was important to me. I didn't start and say, "You've got to reach the pinnacle" but I wanted to be content in what I was doing. Take pride in what I was doing. And if you can do that as a lawyer, that's great. A lot of people do. I just couldn't. I wasn't made that way.

The law is not right for everybody. Although I do think it's an excellent education. I don't regret the three years I spent there. I learned a lot. It's helped me. But as far as being a lawyer, I'm glad I made the decision I did.

• • • • • • • • • • • • •

WHAT YOU SHOULD HAVE LEARNED IN THIS CHAPTER

☐ Your perspective on what making a career transition is like is just that—your perspective. If that perspective isn't so much fun, choose another one. Yes, it can be that simple.

☐ You don't need anyone else's permission but your own to find work you love.

☐ Give yourself permission to try to find what you're longing for. What if you find it?!

Epilogue

You are at the end now. It's time to decide whether you want to take the plunge.

Tell me, what else should I have done?
Doesn't everything die at last, and too soon?
Tell me, what is it you plan to do
with your one wild and precious life?

—Mary Oliver

Endnotes

[1]Bob McDonald and Don E. Hutcheson, *Don't Waste Your Talent: The 8 Critical Steps To Discovering What You Do Best* (Marietta, GA: Longstreet Press, Inc., 2000), xi.

[2]McDonald and Hutcheson, *Don't Waste Your Talent*, 77.

[3]Nella Barkley and Eric Sandburg, *The Crystal-Barkley Guide to Taking Charge of Your Career* (New York: Workman Publishing, 1995), 9.

[4]Barkley and Sandburg, *The Crystal-Barkley Guide*, 10.

[5]Douglas Stone, Bruce Patton, and Sheila Heen, *Difficult Conversations: How to Discuss What Matters Most* (New York: Penguin Books, 2000).

[6]"One of these things is not like the other" is a refrain from a skit on *Sesame Street*, a children's television program. This skit taught children how to distinguish. There were four objects and children would guess which one was different. In law school, Debbie felt like she was the object that was different, as compared to her classmates.

[7]Thanks to coach Cynthia Morris for these questions.

[8]Richard D. Carson, *Taming Your Gremlin: A Guide to Enjoying Yourself* (New York: Harper Perennial, 1983).

[9]Carson, *Taming Your Gremlin*, back cover.

[10]Herminia Ibarra, *Working Identity: Unconventional Strategies for Reinventing Your Career* (Boston: Harvard Business School Press, 2003), front inside cover.

[11]Ibarra, *Working Identity*, 41–42.

[12]Ibarra, *Working Identity*, 1–2.

[13]Barbara Sher, *Refuse to Choose! A Revolutionary Program for Doing Everything that You Love* (New York: Rodale Inc., 2006).

[14]Sher, *Refuse to Choose!*, vii–viii.

[15]Howard Figler and Richard Bolles, *The Career Counselor's Handbook* (Berkeley, CA: Ten Speed Press, 1999), 111–117

[16]Figler and Bolles, *The Career Counselor's Handbook*, 111.

[17]Figler and Bolles, *The Career Counselor's Handbook*, 11.

[18]Figler and Bolles, *The Career Counselor's Handbook*, 114–117.

[19]Judith Wright, *There Must Be More Than This: Finding More Life, Love and Meaning by Overcoming Your Soft Addictions* (New York: Broadway Books, 2003).

[20]Wright, *There Must Be More Than This*, 18.

[21]Laura Whitworth, Henry Kimsey-House, and Phil Sandahl, *Co-Active Coaching: New Skills for Coaching People Toward Success in Work and Life* (Mountain View, CA: Davies-Black Books, 1998), 203.

[22]Thanks to coach Cynthia Morris for this imagery.

[23]Stone, Patton and Heen, *Difficult Conversations*.

[24]This saying, by the way, is also the title of an excellent book by Susan Jeffers. Susan Jeffers, *Feel the Fear and Do It Anyway* (New York: Fawcett Book Group, 1987).

[25]Thanks to the Coaches Training Institute for the Perspective Exercise.

Further Reading

My clients love to read and I love to recommend books! Here are some of the books I frequently share with them. They're not just books on career development but also books on self-development, money, creativity, and self-employment that will help you as you plot and pursue your new career path. I hope you enjoy them as much as my clients have.

Warning: Yes, books can be magical. They can provide practical information and inspire. But they are magical only if you take action after you read them. A book by itself won't change your life. You have to do that.

ON CAREER DEVELOPMENT

Barkley, Nella, and Eric Sandburg. *The Crystal-Barkley Guide to Taking Charge of Your Career*. New York: Workman Publishing, 1995.

Bolles, Richard. *What Color Is Your Parachute? A Practical Manual for Job-Hunters and Career-Changers*. Berkeley, CA: Ten Speed Press, 2007.

Gilman, Cheryl. *Doing Work You Love: Discovering Your Purpose and Realizing Your Dreams*. Chicago: Contemporary Books, 1997.

Ibarra, Herminia. *Working Identity: Unconventional Strategies for Reinventing Your Career*. Boston: Harvard Business School Press, 2003.

Lobenstine, Margaret. *The Renaissance Soul: Life Design for People with Too Many Passions to Pick Just One*. New York: Broadway, 2006.

Lore, Nicholas. *The Pathfinder: How to Choose or Change Your Career for a Lifetime of Satisfaction and Success.* New York: Fireside, 1998.

McDonald, Bob, and Don E. Hutcheson. *Don't Waste Your Talent: The 8 Critical Steps To Discovering What You Do Best.* Marietta, GA: Long Street Press, 2000.

Sher, Barbara. *Refuse to Choose! A Revolutionary Program for Doing Everything that You Love.* New York: Rodale Books, 2006.

ON SELF-DEVELOPMENT
Carson, Richard D. *Taming Your Gremlin: A Guide to Enjoying Yourself.* New York: Harper Perennial, 1983.

Jeffers, Susan. *Feel the Fear and Do It Anyway.* New York: Fawcett Book Group, 1987.

Kabat-Zinn, Jon. *Wherever You Go There You Are: Mindfulness Meditation in Everyday Life.* New York: Hyperion, 2005.

Lindgren, Astrid. *Pippi Longstocking.* New York: Puffin Books, 1997. (I don't know a better role model for living a wild and precious life!)

Stone, Douglas, Bruce Patton, and Sheila Heen. *Difficult Conversations: How to Discuss What Matters Most.* New York: Penguin Books, 2000.

Wright, Judith. *There Must Be More Than This: Finding More Life, Love and Meaning by Overcoming Your Soft Addictions.* New York: Broadway, 2003.

ON MONEY
Dominguez, Joe, and Vicki Robin. *Your Money or Your Life: Transforming Your Relationship with Money and Achieving Financial Independence.* New York: Penguin Books, 1999.

Nemeth, Maria. *The Energy of Money: A Spiritual Guide to Financial and Personal Fulfillment.* New York: Ballantine Wellspring, 1999.

ON CREATIVITY

Cassou, Michele. *Point Zero: Creativity Without Limits.* New York: Jeremy P. Tarcher/Putnam, 2001.

Cassou, Michele, and Stewart Cubley. *Life, Paint and Passion: Reclaiming the Magic of Spontaneous Expression.* New York: Jeremy P. Tarcher/Putnam, 1995.

Edwards, Betty. *The New Drawing on the Right Side of the Brain.* New York: Jeremy P. Tarcher/Putnam, 1999.

Euland, Brenda. *If You Want to Write: A Book about Art, Independence and Spirit.* St. Paul: Graywolf Press, 1987.

Falter-Barns, Suzanne. *How Much Joy Can You Stand? A Creative Guide to Facing Your Fears and Making Your Dreams Come True.* New York: Ballantine Wellspring, 2000.

Goldberg, Natalie. *Writing Down the Bones: Freeing the Writer Within.* Boston: Shambhala Publications, Inc., 2006.

Morris, Cynthia. *Create Your Writer's Life: A Guide to Writing with Joy and Ease.* Boulder: Original Impulse, 2005.

ON SELF-EMPLOYMENT

Winter, Barbara J. *Making a Living without a Job: Winning Ways for Creating Work That You Love.* New York: Bantam Books, 1993.

Zelinski, Ernie J. *Real Success Without a Real Job: There Is No Life Like It!* Berkeley, CA: Ten Speed Press, 2006/2007.

ONLINE

At **www.TheUnhappyLawyer.com**, you can grab a copy of a free *Jumpstart Your Career Transition Kit* and check out additional resources to help you make your transition out of the practice of law and into fulfilling work.

About the Author

Monica Parker is the founder of LeavingTheLaw.com, a career coaching company that helps unhappy lawyers find and pursue fulfilling work outside the practice of law. Prior to starting LeavingTheLaw.com, Monica practiced law for five years at two prestigious law firms in Atlanta, Georgia. She also served as a Lecturer on Law at Harvard Law School, teaching a negotiation course, as well as an executive version of the course through the Program of Instruction for Lawyers at Harvard Law School. Additionally, Monica conducted negotiation training workshops for corporations, nonprofits, colleges, and government agencies in the United States and overseas. Before law school, Monica developed film scripts for Spike Lee at 40 Acres & A Mule Filmworks.

Monica earned her JD from Harvard Law School and a BA cum laude in English and American Literature from Harvard College. She received her coach training from The Coaches Training Institute.

For more information about LeavingTheLaw.com coaching programs and workshops, or to subscribe to Monica's free email newsletter, *Lawyers on the Move*, please go to **www.LeavingTheLaw.com**.